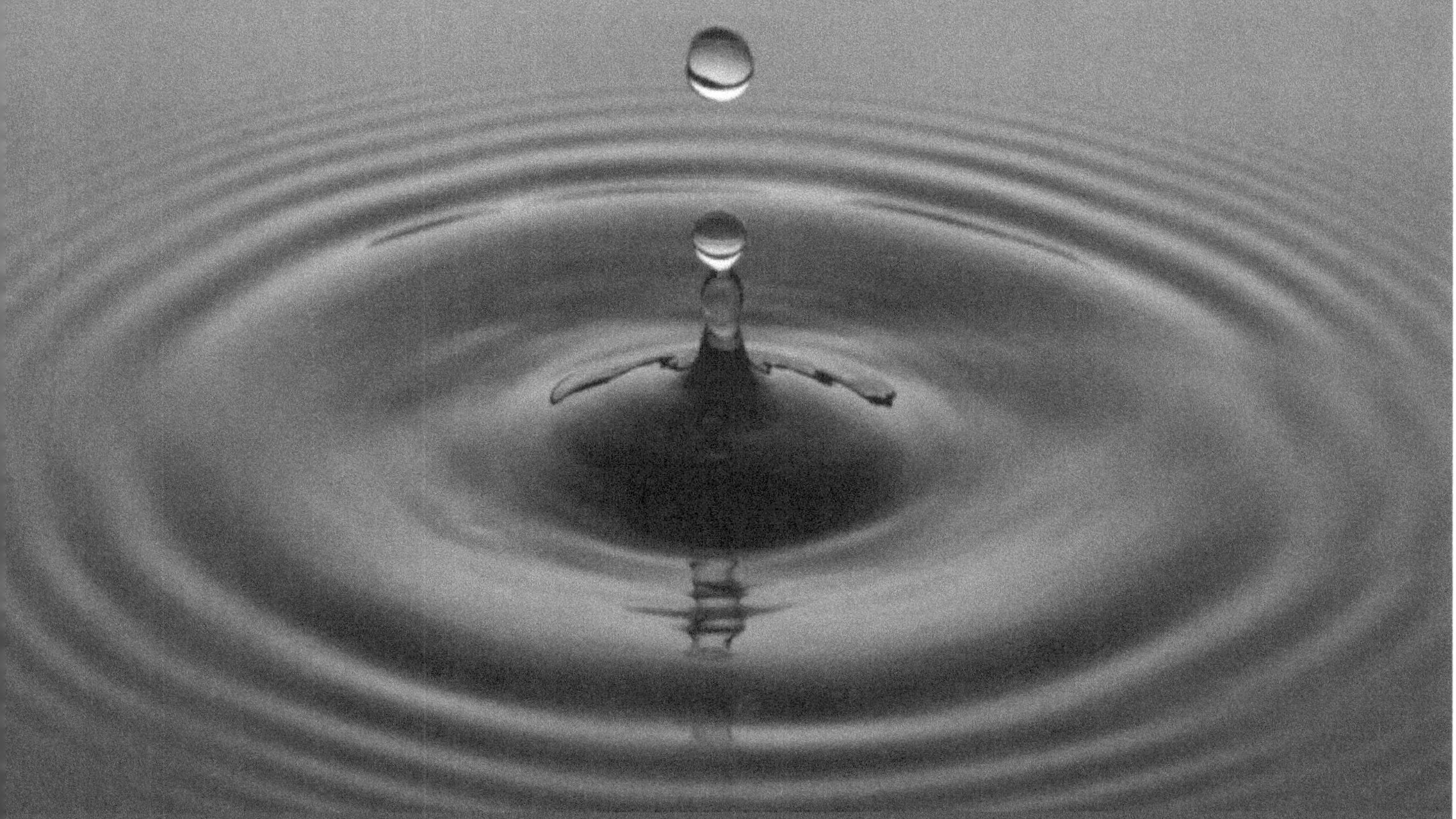

Water Sector-Specific Plan

An Annex to the National Infrastructure Protection Plan

2010

United States
Environmental
Protection Agency

Preface

The 2010 Water Sector-Specific Plan addresses risk-based critical infrastructure protection strategies for drinking water and wastewater utilities, regulatory primacy agencies, and an array of technical assistance partners. The Plan describes processes and activities to enable the protection, and increased resilience, of the sector's infrastructure.

Since publishing the initial Water Sector-Specific Plan in 2007, the Water Sector has made significant and meaningful strides to address the all-hazards risk landscape of today's threat environment, including:

- The Water Sector Coordinating Council's proactive approach to furthering sector goals via the formation of specialized working groups and the development of quality products such as the *Roadmap to a Secure & Resilient Water Sector* and the *Roadmap to Secure Control Systems in the Water Sector*, which is a unified security strategy containing specific goals, milestones, and activities to mitigate cybersecurity risk over the next 10 years;

- The creation and completion of the Nation's first critical infrastructure and key resources resilience-based security metrics initiative under the auspices of the National Infrastructure Protection Plan. In 2008 and 2009, the Water Sector deployed an annual performance metrics process that covered measures for utility and "other actor" agencies, including States, Federal agencies, and Water Sector associations;

- Establishing Water Security Initiative pilots in Cincinnati, Dallas, New York City, Philadelphia, and San Francisco and using information gathered from the initial pilot to publish three interim guidance documents to advise utilities regarding the design, development, deployment, and use of contaminant monitoring and warning systems;

- The promotion, development, and establishment of intrastate mutual aid and assistance agreements, such as Water and Wastewater Agency Response Networks within forty-seven (47) states to foster a utilities-helping-utilities approach to response and recovery efforts following incidents or events; and

- Establishing and exercising regional laboratory response plans under the U.S. Environmental Protection Agency's Water Laboratory Alliance program.

The Water Sector Coordinating Council and Government Coordinating Council, in close coordination with the U.S. Environmental Protection Agency, will continue working to identify gaps and next steps for critical infrastructure protection, resilience, and risk mitigation activities within the Water Sector and across all sectors. As outlined in the *2010 Critical Infrastructure and Key Resources Protection Annual Report for the Water Sector*, this meaningful priority continues to drive the Water Sector's work and attention.

Water Sector Coordinating Council and Government Coordinating Council Letter of Endorsement

Dear Assistant Secretary Keil:

This letter serves as official endorsement of the 2010 Water Sector-Specific Plan, which was developed through a collaborative process within the Water Sector. The Water Sector-Specific Plan represents the blue print to be used for enacting the goals and objectives outlined within the National Infrastructure Protection Plan.

The Water Sector Coordinating Council and Government Coordinating Council express particular appreciation for the responsiveness of the U.S. Environmental Protection Agency and the U.S. Department of Homeland Security in addressing the needs and concerns identified by drinking water and wastewater utility owners and operators throughout this collaborative process. The completion of the revised Water Sector-Specific Plan reinforces the continued importance of the implementation of the partnership model in the National Infrastructure Protection Plan.

The Water Sector-Specific Plan identifies key issues of critical importance to ensuring the continuity of the sector's vital services including:

- Maintaining the integrity of the partnership model. As the Administration considers new and effective ways of protecting the Nation's critical infrastructure, it should continue to enhance the level of interaction between government and non-government stakeholders that occurs within the protective scope of the partnership model. The partnership model creates an atmosphere of collaboration and ultimately increases overall security.

- Enhancing the sector's resilience posture by supporting the Water and Wastewater Agency Response Networks approach to response and recovery. Leveraging the utilities-helping-utilities approach encompassed within each of the Water and Wastewater Agency Response Networks ensures that resiliency is embedded in the operational posture of the sector in an all-hazards approach environment.

- Acknowledging and incorporating Water Sector priorities as outlined in the *"Roadmap to a Secure and Resilient Water Sector,"* a consensus document developed by the Critical Infrastructure Partnership Advisory Council – Water Sector Strategic Planning Working Group. This document illustrates the success possible through effective communication and collaboration efforts between government and non-government partners.

- Furthering preparedness capabilities through the effective sharing of critical all-hazards security-related information via the Water Information Sharing and Analysis Center. As the official communication mechanism for the Water Sector, the Water Information Sharing and Analysis Center should be included, to a greater extent, in planning and preparedness-related initiatives as a means to better inform the sector about key security-related issues, opportunities, and information.

- Acknowledging that the Water Sector has been proactive and compliant with legislative mandates by completing vulnerability assessments and revising emergency response plans in accordance with provisions of the Bioterrorism Act of 2002. The Water Sector-Specific Plan emphasizes the positive changes resulting from the Act and the advances made in the methodologies used by the sector to conduct vulnerability assessments. Utilities use their risk assessments to prioritize security and emergency preparedness improvements by incorporating prevention, detection, response, and recovery concepts into their overall risk management strategy.

We hope the articulation of these points further clarifies our endorsement of the revised Water Sector-Specific Plan. We would encourage the Department of Homeland Security to use this document as a guide to support future enhancements in preparedness, resiliency and overall security in the Water Sector. Both Council Chairs look forward to increased collaboration on all security and resiliency issues that impact the sectors as we continue to build good will and a positive relationship between the Water Sector Coordinating Council and the Government Coordinating Council.

Sincerely,

Don Broussard

Chair
Water Sector Coordinating Council

Patricia A. Tidwell-Shelton

Chair
Government Coordinating Council

Acknowledgments

The U.S. Environmental Protection Agency would like to acknowledge everyone who contributed to the development and finalization of the Water Sector-Specific Plan. In accordance with the U.S. Department of Homeland Security's National Infrastructure Protection Plan partnership model, the U.S. Environmental Protection Agency worked in close collaboration with our Government Coordinating Council, Water Sector Coordinating Council, and other partners to develop this plan. The individuals identified below have devoted significant time, energy, effort, and resources to assist in the development of the 2010 *Water Sector-Specific Plan*.

Carol L. Adams	Allegheny County Sanitary Authority, Pittsburgh, Pennsylvania
Cade Clark	National Association of Water Companies
Cynthia Finley	National Association of Clean Water Agencies
William Komianos	American Water Company
Aaron Levy	Association of Metropolitan Water Agencies
Kevin Morley	American Water Works Association
Charles Murray	Fairfax Water, Fairfax, Virginia
Bridget O'Grady	Association of State Drinking Water Administrators
James Sullivan	Water Environment Federation
Vance Taylor	WaterISAC
Edward Thomas	National Rural Water Association

Table of Contents

List of Figures

List of Tables

Executive Summary

Water Sector infrastructure, which consists of drinking water and wastewater systems, has a long history of implementing programs to provide clean and safe water, thereby protecting public health and the environment across the Nation. For more than thirty (30) years, drinking water and wastewater utilities have been conducting routine daily, weekly, and monthly water quality monitoring under guidance of the Safe Drinking Water Act (SDWA) and Clean Water Act (CWA). Researchers continue to explore ways to improve water quality testing methods. Together, the sector's public health, environmental, security, and resilience efforts form a multi-layered approach to provide clean, safe drinking water and protect public health.

Homeland Security Presidential Directive 7 designates the U.S. Environmental Protection Agency (EPA) as the Federal lead for coordinating and assisting in protecting the Nation's critical Water Sector infrastructure. It is necessary to better protect Water Sector infrastructure to safeguard public health and the economic vitality of our Nation. Malicious acts, natural disasters, and denial of service that affect the sector could result in large numbers of illnesses or casualties, as well as negative economic impacts. Critical services such as firefighting and health care (hospitals), to include other dependent and interdependent sectors such as energy, transportation, and food and agriculture, would suffer damaging effects from a denial of potable water or properly treated wastewater. The initial *Water Sector-Specific Plan* (Water SSP) was released in 2007. The Water SSP has been created to explain how the sector is addressing these matters.

The Water SSP continues to address broad-based critical infrastructure protection implementation strategies for drinking water and wastewater utilities, their regulatory primacy agencies, and the array of technical assistance partners. The plan describes processes and activities to assist drinking water and wastewater utilities as they strive to increase resilience in the sector and be prepared to prevent, detect, respond to, and recover from all hazards. Below is a high-level description of the contents of each Water SSP chapter.

1. Sector Profile and Goals

There are more than one hundred and fifty-three thousand (153,000) public drinking water systems and approximately sixteen thousand and five hundred (16,500) publicly owned treatment works in the United States, most of which are municipal entities. EPA is the Sector-Specific Agency (SSA) for the Water Sector and works with utility owners and operators, as well as representatives from industry associations to ensure that Water Sector protection and resilience strategies are effective and practical for all. In addition, other representatives such as Federal, State, local, tribal, and territorial governments support the sector's planning, protection, and resilience initiatives.

The Water Sector's vision is a secure and resilient drinking water and wastewater infrastructure that provides clean and safe water as an integral part of daily life, ensuring the economic vitality of and public confidence in the Nation's drinking water and wastewater services through a layered defense of effective preparedness and security practices in the sector. The sector's goals in support of the vision are to: (1) sustain protection of public health and the environment; (2) recognize and reduce risks in the Water Sector; (3) maintain a resilient infrastructure; and (4) increase communication, outreach, and public confidence.

2. Identify Assets, Systems, and Networks

The Water Sector is composed of a diverse set of drinking water and wastewater utilities or "assets," which are defined as entire systems for purposes of identification, prioritization, and coordination within the sector. The primary sources for Water Sector asset data are periodic surveys and audits performed by EPA (e.g., collecting operational, financial, and customer data from water and wastewater utilities). By virtue of EPA's approach to meet its mission under the SDWA and CWA, inventories for all Water Sector utilities are updated routinely; as a result, the sector does not require separate or additional data collection efforts to gather asset-level information.

3. Assess Risks

Sector assets are vulnerable to a variety of separate or combined attack methods and natural disasters. Plausible attack methods include explosive devices; contamination in drinking water distribution systems; sabotage of water treatment systems; hazardous material releases; and cyber attacks on Supervisory Control and Data Acquisition (SCADA) systems. Natural incidents such as earthquakes, hurricanes, tornadoes, floods, and pandemics also pose threats to the Water Sector.

To better address risk in the sector, three widely used risk-assessment tools have been adopted by the sector: (1) Risk Assessment Methodology–Water; (2) Security and Environmental Management System emergency response checklist; and (3) Vulnerability Self-Assessment Tool. These tools are being upgraded and revised to improve assessment of emerging threats in the sector. The sector is in the process of developing a fourth tool, a generalized (threat-neutral) consequence analysis tool that will assist the Water Sector in quantifying human health and economic consequences for a variety of asset-threat combinations. The Water Health and Economic Analysis Tool will analyze three different event scenarios – release of a hazardous gas, loss of operating assets, and drinking water distribution system contamination – and provide information that can be used by a utility to perform a more detailed risk assessment.

4. Prioritize Infrastructure

Individual utility owners and operators conduct risk assessments to identify the components of their utilities (e.g., pumps, generators, and SCADA systems) that are of higher consequence and concern in the event of an incident. On a nationwide level, the Water Sector has developed criteria to identify higher-consequence and higher-priority utilities. Four criteria are used to better identify these national level high-consequence assets: (1) population served; (2) amount of chlorine gas stored on site; (3) economic impact; and (4) critical customers served.

5. Develop and Implement Protection Initiatives and Resilience Strategies

Water Sector protection initiatives and resilience strategies are aligned with the sector's goals. Partners work together to guide infrastructure owners and operators toward the most effective strategies for protecting their particular assets. The objective of sector critical infrastructure protection initiatives is to ensure continuity of operations, including procedures designed to prevent, detect, respond to, and recover from all hazards. Such procedures mitigate threats, reduce vulnerability to an attack or other disasters, and minimize consequences, thereby enabling timely and efficient response and restoration after an event.

Owners and operators are responsible for implementing critical infrastructure and key resources (CIKR) protection activities at the utility level, which allows protective programs to be tailored to local geography and conditions, with a focus on the higher-risk situations. Sector partners are implementing initiatives that employ a wide range of protection and resilience approaches such as preparedness training and exercises; technical assistance to high-risk utilities; mutual aid within and across regions; cybersecurity planning; and pandemic preparedness. EPA continues to support implementation of protection initiatives by developing tools, training, technical assistance, guidance, and outreach and communication mechanisms that enhance protection and resilience.

6. Measure Progress

Partners have developed metrics that allow a more thorough evaluation of protection, preparedness, and resilience progress in the sector; these metrics are based on: (1) sector goals, objectives, and supporting strategies which are guided by the *National Infrastructure Protection Plan*; and (2) *Features of an Active and Effective Protective Program for Water and Wastewater Utilities*, a guide developed by the sector. Utilities voluntarily report their progress through the Water Information Sharing and Analysis Center; EPA and State agencies assess performance of government activities. Metrics results are only reported in aggregated form, and individual utility metrics are confidential. Utilities use comparisons against aggregate measures to improve their protection and resilience, and the sector uses aggregate measures to identify improvement priorities.

7. CIKR Protection Research and Development

Sector partners collaboratively plan and execute research and development (R&D) activities. These partners include EPA, the Department of Homeland Security Science and Technology Directorate, States, the Water Research Foundation, the Water Environment Research Foundation, water associations, educational institutions, national research laboratories, public and private research foundations, and other organizations. EPA's *Water Security Research and Technical Support Action Plan* identifies seven priorities that define the protection capabilities needed by the sector. On an annual basis the sector identifies capability gaps that motivate specific R&D projects. Sector representatives also support Federal cross-agency efforts to develop technologies that serve common needs across multiple sectors; mutual solutions are being developed for nine categories of cross-sector R&D needs, such as detection of hazardous agents and cybersecurity countermeasures.

8. Managing and Coordinating Sector-Specific Agency Responsibilities

EPA's responsibility as the Water SSA involves: (1) collaborating and coordinating with all relevant Federal departments and agencies, State and local governments, and the private sector; (2) facilitating the development of risk assessment methodologies for the sector; and (3) encouraging the conduct of risk assessments and the implementation of risk management strategies to protect against and mitigate the effects of all hazards on CIKR. Multiple EPA offices carry out these responsibilities.

To seek input and direction, and to identify gaps and next steps for CIKR protection and resilience activities, EPA coordinates with a variety of partners which include but are not limited to the Water Sector Coordinating Council and the Government Coordinating Council and State, regional, local, territorial, and tribal entities, as well as academia.

Introduction

Safe drinking water is a prerequisite for human activity and properly treated wastewater is vital for preventing disease and protecting the environment. Ensuring continuity of drinking water and wastewater treatment and service is essential to modern life and the Nation's economy. Therefore, it is critical that we protect, as well as increase the resilience of the Nation's drinking water and wastewater infrastructure - collectively known as the Water Sector. In partnership, public and private drinking water and wastewater utilities; national and State associations; State, local, tribal, and territorial governments; research foundations; and Federal agencies have been ensuring the protection and resilience of water services for decades. Water Sector partners collaborate to be better prepared to prevent, detect, respond to, and recover from terrorist attacks and other intentional acts, and natural disasters, otherwise known as the "all-hazards" approach. Throughout the Water Sector-Specific Plan (Water SSP), the terms prevention, detection, response, and recovery are used interchangeably with protection and resilience activity terminology.

Homeland Security Presidential Directive (HSPD)-7 identifies eighteen (18) critical infrastructure and key resources (CIKR) sectors and assigns protection responsibilities to selected Federal Government agencies and departments, or Sector-Specific Agencies (SSAs). The U.S. Environmental Protection Agency (EPA or Agency) is the designated SSA for the Water Sector; this designation recognizes many of the ongoing programs in the Agency that support increasing resilience in the sector, as well as the protection of water quality and drinking water and wastewater infrastructure in an all-hazards context.

The U.S. Department of Homeland Security (DHS) developed a framework to protect all CIKR, which is documented in the *National Infrastructure Protection Plan* (NIPP). This framework provides the unifying structure for integrating current and future CIKR protection efforts into a single national program to achieve the goal of a safer, more secure Nation. DHS is exercising the NIPP risk management framework at the national cross-sector level, and each sector is applying the framework to its unique circumstances.

Figure I-1: NIPP Risk Management Framework

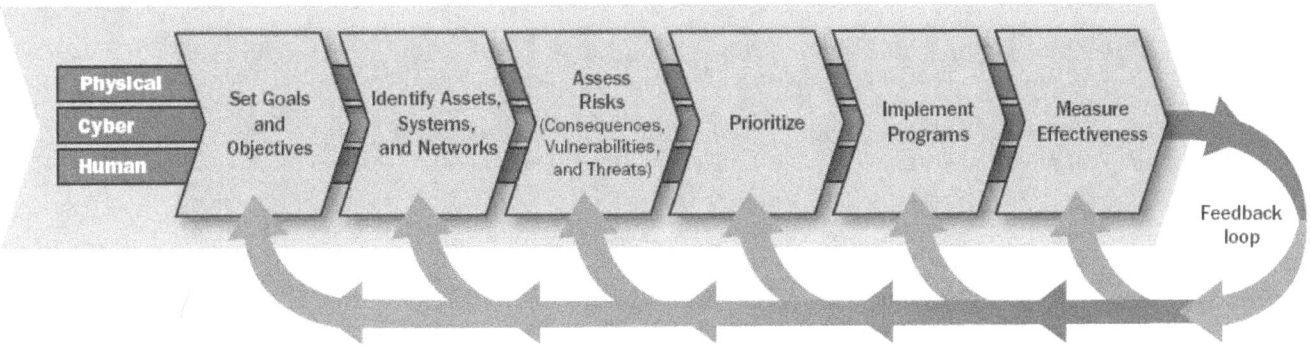

Continuous improvement to enhance protection of CIKR

The Water Sector uses the partnership model, specified in the NIPP, to bring private and public sector participants into the planning and implementation of sector protection. EPA organized a Government Coordinating Council (GCC) including Federal, State, and local entities and owners and operators of water utilities organized the Water Sector Coordinating Council (Water SCC). EPA and these Councils work together and are responsible for planning and implementing the sector's protection activities.

The initial Water SSP was developed in May 2007; this triennial update reflects the sector's progress in each stage of the risk management framework and describes changes in priorities and programs to keep pace with changing risk environments.

1. Sector Profile and Goals

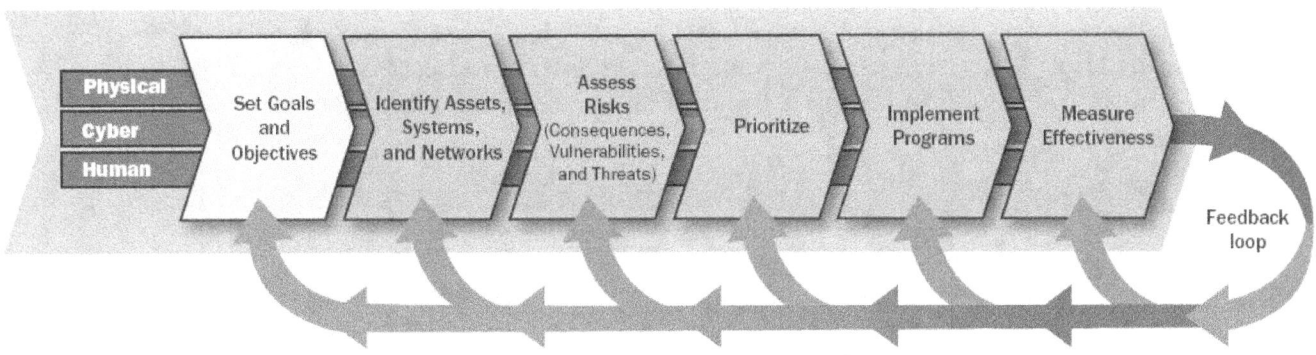

Continuous improvement to enhance protection of CIKR

This chapter includes an overview of the Water Sector—including descriptions of the sector partners; relevant authorities; and the sector's vision and goals. Also covered are the multiple benefits of water security enhancements that may result in improving water quality, while increasing public health and environmental protection.

1.1 Sector Profile

Water Sector utility owners and operators have always had to respond to natural disasters. As a result, emergency response planning is inherent to the industry to ensure continuity of operations and to sustain public health and environmental protection. All-hazards preparedness is manifested in the sector's vision, mission, and goals and aligns with the sector's protection and resilience culture. Many utilities have conducted risk assessments and based on the findings of those assessments, owners and operators have created or updated emergency response plans (ERPs) and implemented numerous protective enhancements. These enhancements include: (1) improving control of access to utilities; (2) expanding physical barriers against vulnerabilities by installing equipment such as backflow prevention devices in pipes and locks on fire hydrants and manholes; (3) increasing control over access, delivery, and storage of chemicals; and (4) hardening cyber network control systems by installing virus-detection software and firewalls, and in some cases by taking control systems offline. Water Sector utilities have also increased their ability to respond to all hazards by: (1) planning for operator and customer protection against influenza pandemics; (2) establishing mutual aid and assistance through Water and Wastewater Agency Response Networks (WARNs); (3) participating in research and development (R&D) programs to improve protection capabilities; (4) improving outreach to the public health sector; (5) enhancing communications with both customers and consumers; and (6) organizing the Water Information Sharing and Analysis Center (WaterISAC) for effective communication for warnings and alerts.

1.1.1 Drinking Water

Drinking water is central to the life of an individual and of society; a drinking water contamination incident or the denial of drinking water services would have far-reaching public health, economic, environmental, and psychological impacts across the Nation. Other critical services such as fire protection, healthcare, and heating and cooling processes would also be disrupted by the interruption or cessation of drinking water service, resulting in significant consequences to the national or regional economies.

The Federal and State governments have long been active in addressing these risks and threats through regulations, technical assistance, research, and outreach programs. As a result, an extensive system of regulations governing maximum contaminant levels of ninety (90) contaminants, construction and operating standards (principally implemented by State regulatory agencies), monitoring, emergency response planning, training, research, and education have been developed to better protect the Nation's drinking water supply and receiving waters.

There are approximately one hundred and fifty-three thousand (153,000) Public Water Systems (PWSs) in the United States. These water systems are categorized according to the number of people they serve, source of water, and whether the same customers are served year-round or on an occasional basis. PWSs provide water for human consumption through pipes or other constructed conveyances to at least fifteen (15) service connections, or serve an average of at least twenty-five (25) people for at least sixty (60) days a year.

Public water systems are defined in three ways: (1) Community Water System (CWS)—a PWS that serves people year-round in their residences; (2) Non-Transient Non-Community Water System (NTNCWS)—a PWS that is not a community water system and regularly serves at least twenty-five (25) of the same people over six (6) months of the year (e.g., schools, factories, office buildings, and hospitals which have their own water systems); and (3) Transient Non-Community Water System (TNCWS)—a PWS that is not a NTNCWS; these systems serve transient consumers. Transient consumers represent individuals who have the opportunity to consume water from a water system but who do not fit the definition of a residential or regular consumer; examples include gas stations or campgrounds where people do not remain for long periods of time. There are more than fifty-one thousand (51,000) CWSs, over eighteen thousand (18,000) NTNCWSs, and approximately eighty-four thousand (84,000) TNCWSs in the United States. See Figure 1-1 for expanded CWS information.

Figure 1-1: Number of Community Water Systems and System Size

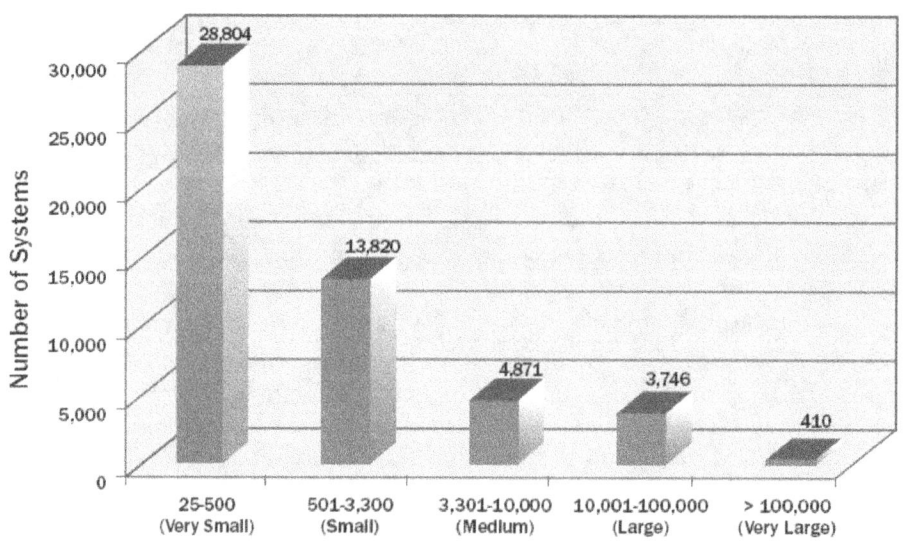

System Size by Population Served

Figure 1-1 illustrates that eighty-three (83) percent of CWS are small or very small systems serving eight (8) percent of the population who get their water from a CWS and seventeen (17) percent of CWS are very large, large, or medium systems, serving ninety-two (92) percent of the population who get water from a CWS.

Under the Safe Drinking Water Act (SDWA), States can request primacy for their drinking water programs. Primacy gives a State the authority to oversee the program within its borders. Forty-nine of the fifty States, the Commonwealth of Puerto Rico, and the Navajo nation have primacy. State agencies that administer drinking water programs are known as primacy agencies. EPA regional offices administer the drinking water program in other entities that do not have primacy including other sovereign tribal nations, Wyoming, the District of Columbia, the Virgin Islands, Guam, American Samoa, and the Commonwealth of Mariana Islands.

Drinking water systems contain many components, as listed below, which are divided into physical, cyber, and human elements.

Physical Elements

- **Water source.** This may be groundwater, surface water, or a combination of the two. The vast majority of CWSs serving fewer than ten-thousand (10,000) people use groundwater as their source. Large CWSs obtain most of their water from surface sources.

- **Conveyance.** To bring water from a remote source to the treatment plant, CWSs may use pipes or open canals; the water may be pumped or gravity-fed.

- **Raw water storage.** Reservoirs or lakes hold water from the source before it is treated; these reservoirs may be in remote or urban areas.

- **Treatment.** A variety of physical and chemical treatments are applied, depending on the contaminants detected in the raw water.

- **Finished water storage.** Treated water is stored before being distributed to customers. In a limited number of cases, treated water is stored in large, uncovered reservoirs that may be vulnerable to attack and contamination.

- **Distribution system.** This network of pipes, tanks, pumps, and valves conveys water to customers. The flow is adjusted so that the proper volume and pressure are delivered when and where needed.

- **Monitoring system.** Most monitoring is conducted for conventional regulated and unregulated contaminants. Some utilities have sensors installed at critical points to monitor a range of physical properties, such as water pressure and water quality.

Cyber Elements

- **Supervisory Control and Data Acquisition (SCADA) system.** Some utilities have electronic networks, often including wireless communication, to link the monitoring system, and controls for the treatment and distribution systems, to a central display in the operations/control room. These systems may also help to automate control of a drinking water utility with monitoring-system readouts serving as inputs for control. SCADA systems are part of integrated control systems essential to operation of drinking water utilities.

Human Elements

- **Employees and contractors.** Drinking water utilities rely on part-time, full-time, and contract employees to manage and operate their facilities. In larger utilities, this may include chemists, engineers, microbiologists, public relations staff, security personnel, and other specialists who are highly trained in their roles individually and as a team. Operators must be appropriately trained and available, typically based on the type, size, and complexity of a utility. Utilities also rely on outside contractors to provide engineering services, laboratory analyses, chemical deliveries, and security services.

Individual drinking water utilities will differ in the types of components used; some utilities may not have all the components listed above (e.g., small utilities may not have SCADA systems).

1.1.2 Wastewater

Disruption of a wastewater treatment utility or service can cause loss of life, economic impacts, and severe public health and environmental impacts. If wastewater infrastructure were to be damaged, the lack of redundancy in the sector might cause denial of service. Regulations, research, and outreach, while extensive, have been aimed mostly at impacts to the environment and public health.

Wastewater is predominantly treated by publicly owned treatment works (POTWs), although there are a small number of private facilities such as industrial plants. The POTWs and privately owned wastewater treatment works that discharge treated effluent into the waters of the United States are subject to regulation under the Clean Water Act's (CWA) National Pollutant Discharge Elimination System (NPDES) program. The administering NPDES body is referred to as the permitting authority. The permitting authority designates uses for all water bodies (e.g., fishing, swimming, and drinking), and then adopts water quality criteria that protect those uses. The permitting authority uses those criteria to set water quality standards for specific bodies of water; it then issues direct discharge permits that limit the concentrations of pollutants in the effluent based on the water quality criteria appropriate to the receiving water body.

There are more than sixteen thousand and five hundred (16,500) POTWs in the United States that collectively provide wastewater service and treatment to over two-hundred and twenty-seven (227) million people and are generally designed to treat domestic sewage. However, POTWs also receive wastewater from industrial (non-domestic) users; these industrial users discharge effluent into a collection system for subsequent treatment at a POTW and are subject to the national pretreatment program. Many States are authorized to administer this program, which ensures that effluent is compatible with the utility's treatment capabilities or, if not, that the effluent is pretreated before being discharged to the collection system. Major and minor dischargers are defined according to a formula that considers the type of industry, flow rate, types of pollutants, and other factors. See Figure 1-2 for expanded POTW information.

Figure 1-2: Number of Publicly Owned Treatment Works and System Size

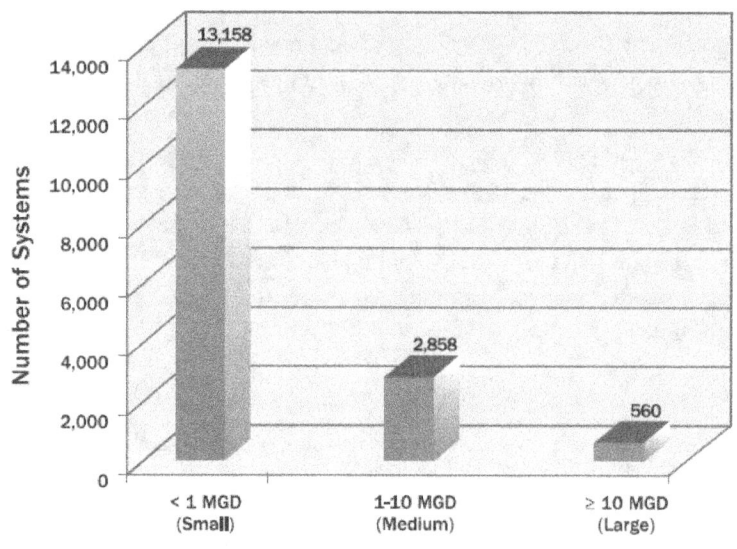

System Size by Flow Rate in Million Gallons per Day

Figure 1-2 illustrates that seventy-nine (79) percent of utilities treat less than one (1) million gallons per day (MGD) and provide wastewater treatment to less than twenty-three (23) million people or approximately ten (10) percent of the population served by POTWs. Utilities that treat more than one MGD provide wastewater treatment to the other ninety (90) percent of the population served or approximately two-hundred and five (205) million people.

As with drinking water, there are relatively few very large wastewater utilities as compared to the number of smaller utilities. There are 382 POTWs that service more than 100,000 people; 2,288 POTWs that service between 10,001 and 100,000 people; 2,598 POTWs that service populations between 10,000 and 3,301; and 11,050 POTWs that service fewer than 3,301 people.

Wastewater utilities contain several components, as listed below, which are divided into physical, cyber, and human elements.

Physical Elements

- **Collection.** A network of pipes that conveys wastewater from the source to the treatment plant. In some older cities, the wastewater and storm water collection systems are integrated in "combined sewer systems," and in wet weather the combined effluent may be discharged directly to the receiving body, bypassing the treatment plant. Wastewater and stormwater collection systems that are not combined are known as separated systems. The wastewater collected and transported in a separated sewer system must be treated prior to discharging to a receiving water body.

- **Raw influent storage.** Raw sewage and industrial effluent stored in tanks or impoundments, generally for the purposes of flow equalization prior to treatment.

- **Treatment.** A variety of physical, biological, and chemical treatment processes applied to plant influent to reduce pollutant levels to concentrations specified in the NPDES permit, in the case of a direct discharger, or other specified discharge limits in the case of an indirect discharger.

- **Treated wastewater storage.** Treated wastewater held in lagoons prior to discharge.

- **Effluent/discharge.** The treated wastewater released to a surface water body, in the case of a direct discharger, or to a POTW collection system in the case of an indirect discharger.

- **Monitoring system.** Sensors installed at critical points to monitor a range of physical properties, such as flow rates and water quality indicators, and to detect levels of contaminants before, during, and after treatment.

Cyber Elements

- **SCADA.** An electronic network, often including wireless communication that links the monitoring system and controls for the collection, treatment, and discharge systems to a central display and operations room. The system may include automated operation of controls based on the monitoring system readouts. A SCADA system may also help to automate control of a wastewater utility, with monitoring system readouts serving as inputs for control. The systems are part of an integrated control system essential to operation of a wastewater utility.

Human Elements

- **Employees and contractors.** Wastewater utilities rely on part-time, full-time, and contract employees to manage and operate their facilities. Larger utilities also may have chemists, engineers, environmental professionals, systems analysts, microbiologists, public relations staff, security personnel, and other specialists who are highly trained in their roles individually and as a team. The training and availability of operators typically is based on the type, size, and complexity of the utility. Wastewater utilities also rely on outside contractors to provide engineering services, laboratory analyses, chemical deliveries, and security services.

Individual wastewater utilities will differ in the types of components used; some utilities may not have all the components listed above (e.g., small utilities may not have SCADA systems).

1.1.3 Key Authorities

A number of governing authorities pertain to the Water Sector; most provide broad environmental authority that may support security-related activities and initiatives. These authorities provide for public health and environmental protection measures; identify and regulate hazardous chemical, radiological, and biological substances; provide for worker safety; ensure that the public receives information about water quality and chemical hazards; and provide enforcement authorities for EPA and State primacy agencies and permitting authorities that implement many of EPA's environmental laws such as the SDWA, CWA, and the Clean Air Act.

Other authorities and directives such as the Homeland Security Act of 2002, HSPDs 7, 8, 9, and 10, and the Public Health Security and Bioterrorism Preparedness and Response Act of 2002 (Bioterrorism Act), address collection of asset-specific information; further promote information sharing and protection; require the conduct of vulnerability assessments and the development of ERPs for certain sizes of CWSs; and encourage or require the identification of protective strategies and implementation of protective programs. Unless otherwise noted, the identified authorities apply to drinking water and wastewater utilities systems; detailed descriptions of authorities and directives that impact the sector are presented in appendix 2.

1.2 CIKR Partners

Water Sector partners along with EPA, State agencies, and other Federal agencies have traditionally shared in the mission to protect public health and the environment. As identified in the NIPP, sector-specific planning and coordination activities are addressed through coordinating councils that are established for each sector. These councils create a structure through which representative groups from all levels of government and the private sector can collaborate or share existing approaches to CIKR protection and work together to advance capabilities.

The Water SCC is composed of water utility managers appointed by the following drinking water and wastewater associations: Association of Metropolitan Water Agencies (AMWA); American Water Works Association (AWWA); Water Research Foundation (WaterRF); National Association of Clean Water Agencies (NACWA); National Association of Water Companies (NAWC); National Rural Water Association (NRWA); Water Environment Federation (WEF); and Water Environment Research Foundation (WERF).

The Water SCC's stated mission is "to serve as a policy, strategy and coordination mechanism and to recommend actions to reduce and eliminate significant homeland security vulnerabilities to the Water Sector through interactions with the Federal Government and other critical infrastructure."

The associations serve as liaisons between the sector's government partners and the broader Water Sector community. The Water SCC interacts on a wide range of sector-specific strategies, policies, activities, and issues and serves as the principal sector policy coordination and planning entity. The Water SCC relies on the WaterISAC and other information-sharing mechanisms that provide operational and tactical capabilities for information sharing and, in some cases, support for incident response activities.

The Federal Government uses the Water SCC as a point-of-entry into the sector to address the entire range of CIKR protection activities, infrastructure protection planning, and issues for the sector. Such activities include planning, development of effective security practices, adoption of protective programs and plans, development of requirements for effective sharing of information, R&D, and cross-sector coordination. The Water SCC meets several times a year.

The Water Sector GCC includes Federal and State government representatives. EPA, as the SSA for the Water Sector, is Chair of the GCC, and the DHS Office of Infrastructure Protection (IP) serves as Co-Chair. The GCC is active in coordinating CIKR strategies, activities, policy, and communications across government entities within each sector. GCC membership consists of key representatives and influential leaders on water protection and resilience issues from Federal and State governments.

Members of the GCC are director-level or equivalent representatives from the U.S. Department of Agriculture's (USDA) Natural Resources Conservation Service; Federal Bureau of Investigation (FBI); U.S. Department of Health and Human Services (HHS); DHS IP; U.S. Department of the Interior (DOI)'s Bureau of Reclamation; EPA; U.S. Army Corps of Engineers (USACE); National Association of Regulatory Commissioners; Association of State Drinking Water Administrators (ASDWA); Association of State and Territorial Health Officials; and State governments. State drinking water programs have provided GCC members since its inception – administrators from Texas and Virginia joined the GCC during 2008. This Council meets on a quarterly basis and may invite others on an ad hoc basis to provide subject matter expertise.

Water SCC and GCC work together and have formed many joint working groups under the auspices of the Critical Infrastructure Partnership Advisory Council (CIPAC). Chapter 8 provides further information on CIPAC, the implementation of the NIPP partnership model, and the development of working groups in the Water Sector.

1.2.1 Other Sector-Specific Agencies

The Water Sector shares dependencies and interdependencies with the other 17 CIKR sectors, principally with Chemical, Energy, Food and Agriculture, Healthcare and Public Health, Transportation Systems, Dams, Information Technology, and Emergency Services Sectors. EPA is responsible for working with the SSAs for these sectors and their sector partners to identify, define, and address interdependencies and joint vulnerabilities; appendix 3 section A3.1 and appendix 4 include more detail on these sector relationships.

1.2.2 CIKR Owners and Operators Including Private and Public Entities

The Water Sector is a partnership of public and private drinking water and wastewater utilities; national and State associations; State, local, and tribal governments; research foundations; and Federal agencies that, in concert, have been ensuring the protection and resilience of water services for decades. Partners collaborate to be better prepared to prevent, detect, respond to, and recover from all-hazards events. Appendix 3 section A3.2 includes more detail on the entities that form this partnership.

1.2.3 U.S. Department of Homeland Security

EPA continually communicates and coordinates with DHS on Water Sector security; the Agency works with DHS in implementing various presidential directives, executive orders, and statutes. To improve these efforts, EPA has designated a liaison to DHS; the liaison helps to coordinate and share information between DHS, EPA, and sector partners as it pertains to CIKR protection. DHS uses its Partnership and Outreach Division to serve as the primary portal to communicate and coordinate with EPA and other SSAs on issues involving CIKR protection and implementation of the NIPP and the SSPs.

EPA's National Homeland Security Research Center (NHSRC) coordinates regularly with the DHS Science and Technology Directorate (S&T) to exchange information on research needs and to discuss R&D priorities and needs for a wide range of security-related research areas.

EPA also coordinates with DHS to provide insight on the vulnerability and consequence issues that directly impact Water Sector utilities. A better understanding of vulnerability and consequence allows DHS to interpret water-related threat information (classified and unclassified) and to develop and distribute timely and accurate threat-warning products that are relevant to the sector.

1.2.4 Other Federal Departments and State, Local, Tribal, and Territorial Governments

The Water Sector also interacts with other Federal department and agencies regarding Water Sector protection programs including but not limited to: (1) the U. S. Department of State (DOS) for cross-border protection issues; (2) DOI for dams, reservoirs, and water quality assessments; and (3) the FBI and the other U.S. Intelligence Community elements on threat information sharing; appendix 3 section A3.3 includes more information on these Federal Government relationships.

As noted previously, EPA depends heavily on State drinking water primacy agencies and the wastewater permitting authorities that implement the SDWA and CWA. Because all but one drinking water and most wastewater programs are delegated to the States, EPA works with them to ensure implementation of programmatic, protection, and resilience-related initiatives.

In addition to Federal regulatory responsibilities, States also have their own initiatives and priorities; State programs maintain inventories of drinking water and wastewater facilities, regularly inspect these utilities, provide technical assistance and training, maintain laboratory and operator certification programs, and monitor compliance by reviewing analytical results. States review and approve plans and specifications for new and expanded drinking water and wastewater facilities and may take enforcement actions as needed.

Because of the primacy and permitting relationship with the States, EPA works very closely with the two organizations that represent State drinking water and wastewater programs: (1) ASDWA represents drinking water agencies in the States, District of Columbia, Territories, commonwealths, and tribes of the United States; and (2) the Association of State and Interstate Water Pollution Control Administrators (ASIWPCA) represents wastewater programs in the same jurisdictions.

EPA is coordinating its protection and resilience efforts and initiatives with these State, local, and tribal governments, as well as public and private entities that represent the Water Sector. This coordination includes facilitating meetings, seeking input on sector security concerns and issues, and raising security awareness. Many of these entities are used as conduits to get information and training opportunities to utilities.

EPA communicates with these associations regularly and meets frequently with State work groups to discuss issues and set priorities. The Agency also meets with association members at their annual conferences, meetings, and special events such as security workshops, and EPA regional offices frequently communicate with State programs.

Through this extensive network, EPA can communicate quickly and efficiently with State, local, and tribal governments, as well as private and public entities. The broad perspectives and extensive memberships of many of these organizations allow feedback and input on interdependencies, and provide a basis for establishing security priorities in the Water Sector that complement actions taken at the local level. EPA communicates with these organizations through conference calls and meetings, and solicits their input on security policy decisions.

1.2.5 Regional Coalitions

In an effort to coordinate CIKR protection efforts within geographic areas and across jurisdictional boundaries, the Regional Consortium Coordinating Council (RCCC) was formed in 2008. The RCCC provides a means for DHS to interact with over 20 coalitions and partnerships across the country. The mission of the RCCC is to strengthen regional collaborations that enhance protection, response, recovery, and resilience of the Nation's CIKR. The RCCC fosters collaboration among regional consortia so that best practices, lessons learned, and other means of support can be shared; and supports the Federal policy process so that protection and resilience efforts take geographic regions and sector interdependencies into account.

Although the Water Sector is not currently working with the RCCC on any joint protection efforts, due to their cross-sector and regional focus, the sector is open to participating in future projects with the RCCC.

1.2.6 International Organizations and Foreign Countries

Some Water Sector CIKR assets within the United States are interconnected with Mexico or Canada's infrastructure, supporting the economies on both sides of the border. The NIPP strategy for international CIKR protection and coordination is focused on instituting effective cooperation with international CIKR partners, as well as high-priority cross-border protective programs.

Specific protective actions are developed through the sector planning process and specified in SSPs; they address cross-sector and global issues such as cybersecurity and foreign investment.

The Water Sector recognizes the need to identify international water assets that relate to U.S. assets as well as to establish protocols for sharing information. Efforts are also needed to improve international coordination on CIKR activities and understand potential impacts on homeland security. DHS and DOS serve as the lead agencies that work with the international community on this matter; the Water Sector will continue to support such activities.

1.3 Sector Goals and Objectives

Water Sector Vision Statement:

A secure and resilient drinking water and wastewater infrastructure that provides clean and safe water as an integral part of daily life, ensuring the economic vitality of and public confidence in the Nation's drinking water and wastewater service through a layered defense of effective preparedness and security practices in the sector.

EPA's Water Security Mission Statement:

To provide national leadership in developing and promoting programs that enhance the sector's ability to prevent, detect, respond to and recover from all hazards.

1.3.1 Elements and Characteristics of Sector Goals

The sector's vision and mission are the foundations for its goals. Figure 1-3 illustrates how the mission and vision statements support development of goals, objectives, and milestones, ultimately leading to measurement of progress. These elements continue to be used by the sector to develop and implement protective programs and measure progress as discussed in subsequent chapters of the Water SSP.

Figure 1-3: Sector Strategic Planning Framework

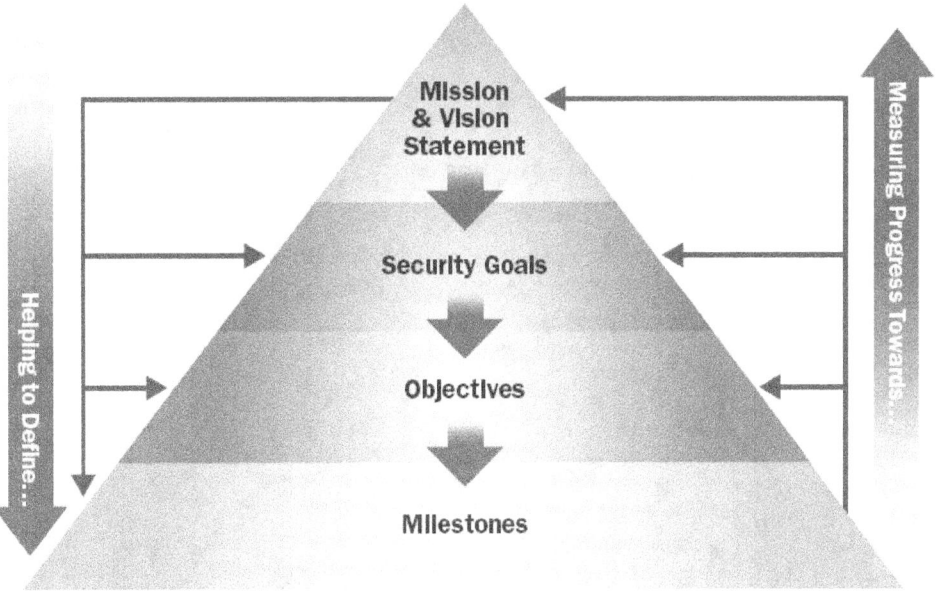

Protection and resilience activities are designed to prevent, detect, respond to, and recover from all hazards. These actions reduce vulnerabilities, minimize consequences, and enable timely, efficient response and restoration following an event. Based on the Water Sector's vision statement, four overarching strategic goals have been established, as shown in Table 1-1.

Table 1-1: Water Sector Goals

Sector Goals	
Goal 1	Sustain protection of public health and the environment.
Goal 2	Recognize and reduce risk.
Goal 3	Maintain a resilient infrastructure.
Goal 4	Increase communication, outreach, and public confidence.

The sector has identified a list of objectives that support each goal; these goals and objectives focus on the concepts of prevention, detection, response, and recovery. They also satisfy the sector's vision and the NIPP framework, and they guide EPA's strategic planning process for sector protection and resilience. The goals and objectives presented in Table 1-2 are at various stages of planning and implementation.

Table 1-2: Water Sector Goals and Objectives

Goal 1	Sustain protection of public health and the environment.
The Nation relies on sustained availability of safe drinking water and on treatment of wastewater to maintain public health and environmental protection. To better protect public and environmental health, the Water Sector works to ensure the continuity of both drinking water and wastewater services.	
Objective 1	Encourage integration of security concepts into daily business operations at utilities to foster a security culture.
Objective 2	Evaluate and develop surveillance, monitoring, warning, and response capabilities to recognize and address all-hazards risks at Water Sector systems that affect public health and economic viability.
Objective 3	Develop a nationwide laboratory network for water quality protection that integrates Federal and State laboratory resources and uses standardized diagnostic protocols and procedures, or develop a supporting laboratory network capable of analyzing threats to water quality.
Goal 2	**Recognize and reduce risk.**
With an improved understanding of the vulnerabilities, threats, and consequences, owners and operators of utilities can continue to thoroughly examine and implement risk-based approaches to better protect, detect, respond to, and recover from all hazards.	
Objective 1	Improve identification of vulnerabilities based on knowledge and best available information, with the intent of increasing the sector's overall protection posture.
Objective 2	Improve identification of potential threats through knowledge base and communications—with the intent of increasing the overall protection posture of the sector.
Objective 3	Identify and refine public health and economic impact consequences of manmade or natural incidents to improve utility risk assessments and enhance the sector's overall protection posture.

Goal 3	Maintain a resilient infrastructure.

The Water Sector will investigate how to optimize continuity of operations to ensure the economic vitality of communities and the utilities that serve them. Response and recovery from an incident in the sector will be crucial to maintaining public health and confidence.

Objective 1	Emphasize continuity of drinking water and wastewater services as it pertains to utility emergency preparedness, response, and recovery planning.
Objective 2	Explore and expand implementation of mutual aid agreements/compacts in the Water Sector. The sector has significantly enhanced its resilience through agreements among utilities and States; increasing the number and scope of these will further enhance resilience.
Objective 3	Identify and implement key response and recovery strategies. Response and recovery from an incident in the sector will be crucial to maintaining public health and confidence.
Objective 4	Increase understanding of how the sector is interdependent with other critical infrastructure sectors. Sectors such as Healthcare and Public Health and Emergency Services are largely dependent on the Water Sector for their continuity of operations, while the Water Sector is dependent on sectors such as Chemical and Energy for continuity of its operations.

Goal 4	Increase communication, outreach, and public confidence.

Safe drinking water and water quality are fundamental to everyday life. An incident in the Water Sector could have significant impacts on public confidence. Fostering and enhancing the relationships between utilities, government, and the public can mitigate negative perceptions in the face of an incident.

Objective 1	Communicate with the public about the level of protection and resilience in the Water Sector and provide outreach to ensure the public's ability to be prepared for and respond to a natural disaster or manmade incident.
Objective 2	Enhance communication and coordination among utilities and Federal, State, and local officials and agencies to provide information about threats.
Objective 3	Improve relationships among all Water Sector partners through a strong public-private partnership characterized by trusted relationships.

These goals and objectives will continue to drive development and implementation of protective programs described in chapter 5 and measures of progress described in chapter 6.

1.3.2 Process to Establish Sector Goals

To develop the original Water SSP, the sector established a collaborative and interactive process for developing Water Sector goals that included involvement with the Water SCC, GCC, DHS, and other sector partners. That process has continued and matured since the original Water SSP, with the Water SSC and the GCC providing greater detail about sector priorities and programs to achieve the goals.

While there are many activities working toward the Sector's vision and goals, guiding the immense scale and scope of activities among industry and government has been a significant challenge. In October 2009, the Water SCC released the Water SCC *Roadmap to a Secure & Resilient Water Sector* (hereinafter referred to as the Strategic Roadmap), which reflects the Water SCC's needs and priorities for reducing infrastructure risk.

The Strategic Roadmap established a strategic framework that: (1) defines a consensus-based strategy that articulates the priorities of industry and government in the Water Sector to manage and reduce risk; (2) produces an actionable path forward for the Water SCC, GCC, and sector partners to improve the security and resilience of the Water Sector over the near term (one to two years) and mid term (three to five years); (3) directly guides new product development, creates a shared understanding of priorities to avoid unpleasant surprises, collectively advocates sector priorities, and recognizes institutional constraints and different accountabilities; and (4) encourages extensive engagement among all key stakeholders to strengthen public-private partnerships and accelerate security advances throughout the Water Sector.

The Strategic Roadmap identifies the top three security priorities as: (1) developing templates for detection, response, and recovery plans; (2) updating ERPs; and (3) increasing public and political understanding of the impact of denial-of-service to facilitate rate recovery of resilience and continuity initiatives.

The Strategic Roadmap is a living document. By working together to develop this Strategic Roadmap, the sector has leveraged a broad range of operational and infrastructure protection experience to identify the most pressing sector needs and prioritize actions that industry and government can take to begin immediately enhancing water security and resilience.

1.4 Value Proposition

Efficiently and effectively protecting the physical, human, and cyber elements of the Water Sector necessitates significant contributions from all sector partners. These contributions require time and energy and, in many circumstances, financial and other resources from the owners and operators of CIKR. While the expenses for Federal CIKR partners are typically funded through governmental appropriations, the non-Federal CIKR partners for the most part do not receive such funding. However, as traditional stewards of public health and the environment, States and drinking water and wastewater utilities work to ensure continuity of operations to sustain protection of public health and the environment. This concept manifests itself in the Water Sector's vision statement and its goals, and the need to be prepared for all hazards aligns with the sector's culture.

Water Sector owners and operators and other CIKR partners continue to enhance protection and resilience of the Nation's water infrastructure for the basic benefit of ensuring continuity of their services. These activities have multiple benefits, such as: (1) the satisfaction of contributing to protection of the Nation, the American people, national economy, and American way of life; (2) the ability to provide input to the design of Federal, State, and local programs that may better protect and prepare utilities against all hazards; (3) the ability to influence the allocation of Federal, State, and local funds and other resources that may help secure the Water Sector's infrastructure; (4) the receipt of timely, accurate, and useful information on threats to the sector, as well as receipt of protective best practices and assessment methodologies and other information and tools that can help utility owners and operators better assess and protect their systems and investments from all hazards; (5) the improvement of relationships with EPA, DHS, and other government agencies on security and emergency preparedness; (6) the ability to influence the type of environment through which Water Sector security and emergency preparedness are promoted; and (7) the enhanced cybersecurity postures that can prevent business interruption or loss or misuse of sensitive information.

These mutual benefits enhance Water Sector owners' and operators' ability to prevent, detect, respond to, and recover from all hazards and increase preparedness and resilience to better ensure continuity of services from utilities.

2. Identify Assets, Systems, and Networks

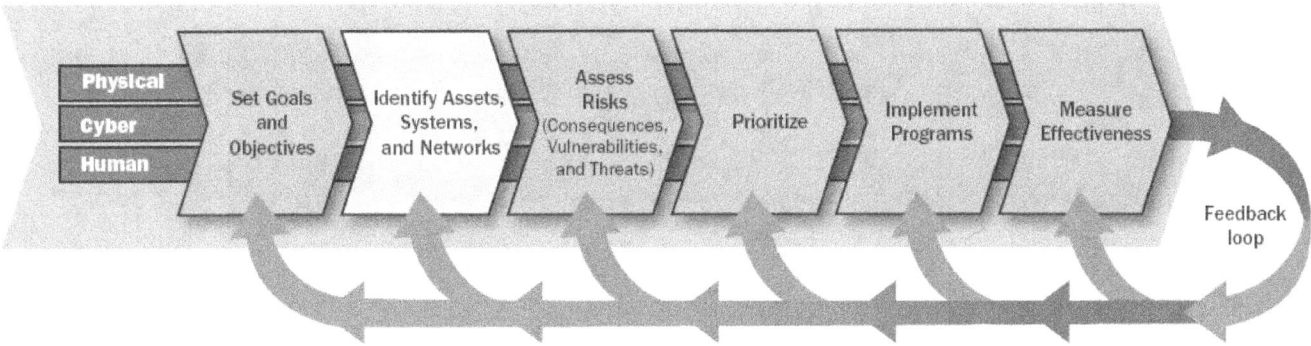

Continuous improvement to enhance protection of CIKR

This chapter includes information on the processes for defining, collecting, verifying, and updating Water Sector asset information. The primary sources for Water Sector asset data are periodic surveys and censuses performed by EPA collecting operational, financial, and customer data from water and wastewater utilities.

2.1 Defining Information Parameters

The Water Sector is composed of a diverse set of drinking water and wastewater utilities; sector "assets" are defined as entire systems for purposes of identification, prioritization, and coordination. Owners and operators are responsible for conducting risk assessments of their utility to identify components (e.g., pumps, generators, and SCADA systems) that if lost or damaged, due to manmade or natural events, could adversely affect the utility's operation; threaten public health or the environment; disrupt the operations of other, interdependent CIKR sectors; or have significant negative economic impacts on a locality or region. Sector partners continue to work together to develop more robust threat, vulnerability, and consequence information in order to assist utility owners and operators to identify their most critical asset components.

2.1.1 Identifying Cyber Infrastructure

In an October 2007 report, the U.S. Government Accountability Office (GAO) evaluated the cybersecurity programs of all CIKR sectors. In the report, GAO concluded that the Water Sector was effectively identifying cyber assets and related interdependencies. Recognizing the risks to Water Sector cyber systems, partners recently developed the *Roadmap to Secure Control Systems in the Water Sector* (hereinafter referred to as the Cybersecurity Roadmap). The Cybersecurity Roadmap is a unified security strategy containing specific goals, milestones, and activities to mitigate cyber risk over the next ten years. As part of the Cybersecurity

Roadmap process, the sector identified the components of SCADA systems used in Water Sector utilities—these components include the central control station, human-machine interface, local processors, instruments, and operating equipment. There is also a workforce component to cyber infrastructure—the downsizing of the sector workforce has resulted in a critical dependency on certain highly skilled human resources. The Cybersecurity Roadmap anticipates that critical cyber assets will be identified based on potential consequences and that utility cybersecurity enhancements will therefore focus on those most consequential components. As of fall 2009, the Water Sector is following the path set forth in the Cybersecurity Roadmap and has hosted a series of SCADA centric cybersecurity workshops around the country. Led by a team of instructors from DHS, the workshops include: (1) a briefing on the Cybersecurity Roadmap to review the goals, milestones, and information on roles, responsibilities, and relationship models for information technology and industrial control systems; (2) an overview of cyber risks and threats to utility-based industrial control systems; (3) concrete and easy-to-understand mitigation strategies for securing industrial control systems; and (4) a demonstration and instruction on the DHS mitigation and self-assessment tools.

2.2 Collecting and Updating Infrastructure Information

By virtue of EPA's approach to meeting its mission under the SDWA and CWA, inventories for Water Sector assets are updated routinely. Therefore, EPA and its sector partners do not plan to initiate additional asset data collection efforts beyond current levels. EPA works with its sector partners to support the regular update of Water Sector asset and infrastructure data and reduce the burden of reporting by using advanced data collection technologies. When deemed necessary for better protecting and increasing the resilience of the sector, partners will ensure more frequent updates of vital data. Inventory processes are described below.

2.2.1 Drinking Water Data

Safe Drinking Water Information System (SDWIS). This national database contains a complete inventory of all PWSs. Data relevant to security include system type (e.g., CWS, TNCWS), service population, source water, detailed location information, treatment, and type of area served (e.g., residential, school, mobile home park). Drinking water utilities report data to States, which collect and upload the information electronically every quarter to the SDWIS database.

Drinking Water Infrastructure Needs Survey. Data are collected from a survey of more than three thousand (3,000) PWSs and include a census of all utilities serving populations of one hundred thousand (100,000) or more and a statistical sample of those serving smaller populations. The survey, which began in 1995, is updated every four years since 1995. Extensive data on needed upgrades, replacement, or construction of new assets are collected; because the survey focuses on utilities with needs, it gives less than complete information on all assets in place.

CWS Survey. The quadrennial survey is a national statistical sample intended to provide estimates of the operating and financial characteristics of CWSs by size category, water source, and ownership type. Only CWSs serving more than one hundred thousand (100,000) people are surveyed. Information relevant to water security includes water interconnections with other systems, volumes drawn and stored, capacity and production of each treatment plant, treatment in place, use of a SCADA system, and length and age of distribution mains. Maps and other sensitive information are not publicly available in the CWS survey database.

2.2.2 Wastewater Data

Permit Compliance System (PCS). This national database contains information on POTWs and industrial dischargers. The database is updated quarterly by the permitting authority; information pertinent to security includes average permitted flow, type of industrial activity that produces the waste stream (in the case of industrial dischargers), treatment type (e.g., primary, secondary, and tertiary), and details on the water body that receives the discharge; PCS is readily accessed by the public via the Internet.

Clean Watersheds Needs Survey. The survey represents only municipal dischargers permitted by NPDES; there is no comparable system for reporting infrastructure needs for industrial dischargers. The data are collected and entered into EPA's database by the permitting authority. This survey has been updated every four years since its inception and contains information on needed upgrades, replacements, and expansions of infrastructure such as treatment plants and sewers. The survey also collects design information such as treatment plant capacity and length of sewer pipe.

2.3 Verifying Infrastructure Information

Data verification and update is an ongoing process; much of the data collected by EPA that pertains to the Water Sector is subject to verification and validation protocols. EPA's databases and surveys have well-established quality control and verification procedures for data collection and data entry, including data screening, double-key entry, and logic checks; therefore, there is no need for new data collection efforts to identify drinking water and wastewater assets. If additional data verification is required, it will be necessary to involve individual asset owners and operators.

Obstacles remain regarding the collection, verification, validation, storage, protection, sharing, and tracking of sector security information and measurements; the provisions of the Paperwork Reduction Act will also impact data collection efforts by Federal agencies. To provide and protect information that pertains to the Water Sector's security status, the sector works to improve upon existing mechanisms for providing information to utility owners and operators, as well as the collection of consequence analysis, vulnerability, and threat information. Working with DHS, EPA and its sector partners will continue to explore mechanisms to share and receive voluntarily submitted sensitive Water Sector data.

3. Assess Risks

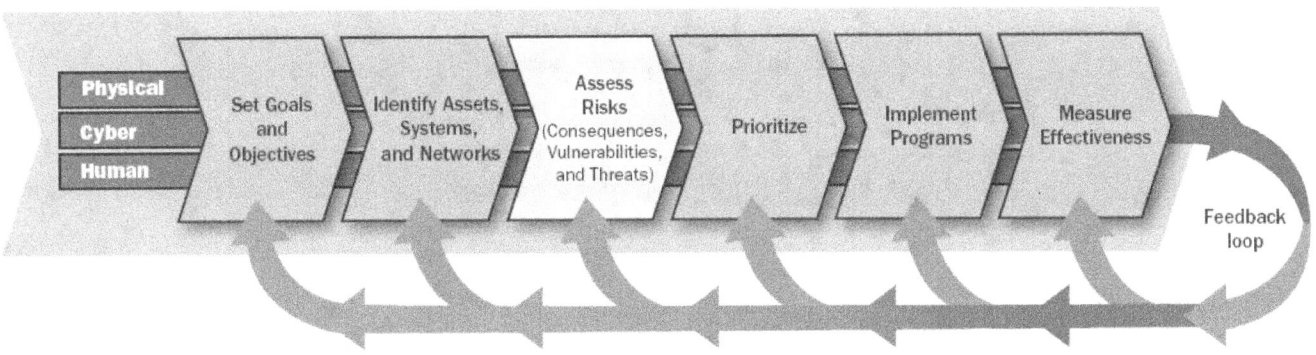

Continuous improvement to enhance protection of CIKR

This chapter includes information on the sector's approach for assessing risk including initial screening of assets, risk assessment methodologies, the importance of interdependencies with other sectors, and risk assessment improvement initiatives.

3.1 Use of Risk Assessment in Sector

Risk is a measure of potential public health and economic harm that encompasses threat, vulnerability, and consequences. Conducting risk assessments in the Water Sector is a fundamental and effective security practice for protecting drinking water and wastewater assets. Water Sector partners have developed a comprehensive all-hazards program that includes a suite of risk assessment tools, training, research initiatives, outreach materials, and technical and financial assistance to help drinking water and wastewater utilities identify and better protect their key components. The initiatives and actions described in this section directly support each of the sector's goals, particularly Goal 2: Recognize and Reduce Risk in the Water Sector.

Because of the diversity of assets in the Water Sector (e.g., size, treatment complexity, disinfection practices, geographic location), a multitude of all-hazard risk assessment methodologies have been developed and are used by sector owners and operators. These tools address the full range of utility components, including the physical plant (physical); employees (human); information technology / SCADA and communications (cyber); and customers.

Risk assessments include one or more factors, as shown in Figure 3-1:

• **Consequence Analysis**, which is the estimate of the potential public health and economic impacts that a successful attack could cause;

- **Threat Analysis**, which estimates the likelihood that a particular target, or type of target, will be selected for attack based on intent and capability of an adversary. Threats from natural events (e.g., hurricanes, earthquakes) are often called hazards; and

- **Vulnerability Assessment**, which identifies weaknesses in an asset design, implementation, or operation that can be exploited by an adversary.

Figure 3-1: Calculating Risk

$$\text{Risk (R)} = f\{\text{Consequence (C), Threat (T), Vulnerability (V)}\}$$

The Water Sector continues to encourage and support the conduct and revision of risk assessments and ERPs by drinking water and wastewater utilities of all sizes. This support is provided through development of risk assessment tools, training, and technical assistance that address the full spectrum of all-hazards risk assessment.

Full risk assessments include all three factors (C, V, and T), resulting in a comprehensive, systematic, and defensible assessment of an asset that drives integrated risk reduction activities. Assessments are conducted at the asset level by owners and operators and are based on local conditions, threats, and other factors; approaches to and the results of an assessment may vary for each type of asset.

3.2 Screening Infrastructure

The different risk assessment methodologies developed for use by utility owners and operators allow for the choice of the most applicable methodology to a utility's security requirements depending on utility size, treatment method, and population served. The application of "level" criteria—the identification of higher-consequence assets—allows a utility owner or operator to quickly assess terrorism-related security concerns to their asset and determine what level of rigor to apply when conducting a risk assessment. More details on the level criteria identification process are provided in chapter 4.

3.3 Assessing Consequences

Drinking water contamination, the denial of drinking water and wastewater services, and prolonged service interruptions to dependent or interdependent assets and other critical customers (e.g., the Energy, Chemical, Information Technology, Healthcare and Public Health, Banking and Finance, and Food and Agriculture Sectors), would likely have far-reaching negative public health, economic, and psychological impacts.

3.3.1 Public Health Effects

Serious health impacts could result from the introduction of contaminants into a drinking water system; these impacts could vary depending on the type of substance and the amount of time before contamination is detected. The impact to the Healthcare and Public Health Sector could be significant as people seek medical evaluation for possible exposure to a harmful agent. Contaminated drinking water could pose a public health hazard from ingestion, inhalation, or absorption through the skin. Any denial of drinking water or wastewater service could pose health effects from the lack of clean and potable water or the inability to dispose of wastewater.

3.3.2 Economic Impacts

The economic impacts of a terrorist attack or natural disaster on drinking water or wastewater utilities could be significant for businesses and infrastructure in a community or region. Impacts could be lost productivity and cascading effects on other critical sectors. Other economic impacts to consider are loss of revenue from local businesses (e.g., restaurants and hotels) and costs associated with the decontamination or repair of Water Sector utility treatment, distribution, and collection infrastructure.

- **Lost productivity:** Denial of drinking water and wastewater utility services—whether the result of a contamination incident, physical attack, or cyber attack—would have cascading effects, as many hospitals, schools, and commercial and industrial businesses would be forced to close. Loss of service and loss of sanitation could require evacuation of the impacted area until service could be restored. Firefighters also would have difficulty responding to emergencies until full service could be restored.

- **Infrastructure damage:** Repair of damaged infrastructure could, in some cases, be prolonged depending on the availability of industrial equipment. The effects of an attack on the provision of services could be prolonged as replacement equipment and infrastructure are obtained and installed—especially in systems with equipment designed specifically for the utility that would need to be custom-built.

3.3.3 Psychological Impacts/Governance Impacts

Even if an attempt to contaminate a drinking water utility did not result in fatalities or large numbers of casualties, terrorists still could do harm by promoting fear and panic in the impacted community and in concerned communities across the Nation. Officials seeking to identify the contaminant and the extent of contamination could issue a "do not drink" or "do not use" order. Pending determination of the contaminant and evaluation of the risk, fears of the unknown contaminant's effects could grow and undermine public confidence in the ability to ensure safe water supplies. Restoring public confidence after a contamination event, even with appropriate decontamination, could require significant effort. A prolonged water incident could affect the Federal and/or State and local governments' ability to maintain order, deliver minimum essential public services, ensure public heath and safety, and carry out national security missions.

3.3.4 Interdependencies and Dependencies

Interdependencies within the Water Sector and among the other CIKR sectors must be considered when discussing consequences; these interdependencies may have local, regional, or national implications. By definition, infrastructure interdependencies transcend individual sectors and may transcend individual companies. Further, interdependencies vary in scale and complexity, ranging from local linkages (e.g., municipal water supply systems and local emergency services) to regional linkages (e.g., electric power coordinating councils), national linkages (e.g., interstate natural gas and transportation systems), and international linkages (e.g., communications, banking, and financial systems). Each link in Water Sector infrastructure has important, and potentially different, spatial, temporal, and utility characteristics. These dependencies and interdependencies are taken into consideration when utilities conduct their consequence analyses as part of the risk assessment process.

Interdependencies historically have been considered to be either physical or geographic. For example, the Water Sector and the Energy Sector are integrally and often physically linked—water and wastewater utilities need power to operate pumps and treatment operations, while electric power facilities often depend on water for cooling equipment and processes. Geographic interdependencies arise when infrastructure components (e.g., water pipelines, conveyance lines, gas pipelines, and telecommunications cables) share common corridors, thus increasing the vulnerabilities to and consequences of all hazards.

The increased use of automated monitoring and control systems and SCADA systems has increased the interdependencies among infrastructure. Furthermore, greater use of the open market for buying and selling some infrastructure commodities and services has also increased the interdependencies. Preparing for and responding to incidents involving critical infrastructure requires that interdependent events and impacts be properly identified and assessed. See appendix 4 for a list of Water

Sector interdependencies and dependencies. The Water Sector has engaged with all partners including DHS' Cross-Sector Cyber Security Working Group and the Industrial Control System Joint Working Group to enhance identification of cyber interdependencies between sectors.

Water is an unusual commodity that is continually used and reused. The water taken in by a supplier may have been treated and discharged by a user upstream; this situation creates a unique *intradependency* among individual water or wastewater utilities. If an upstream wastewater discharger is not sufficiently prepared for emergencies, utility representatives might release untreated or insufficiently treated water into a river that is the raw water source for a downstream drinking water supplier.

Figure 3-2 illustrates some of the interdependencies of drinking water and wastewater infrastructure with the infrastructure and services of other sectors, such as transportation, health care, natural gas, petroleum liquids, communications, emergency management services, and electric power.

Figure 3-2: Interdependencies with the Water Sector

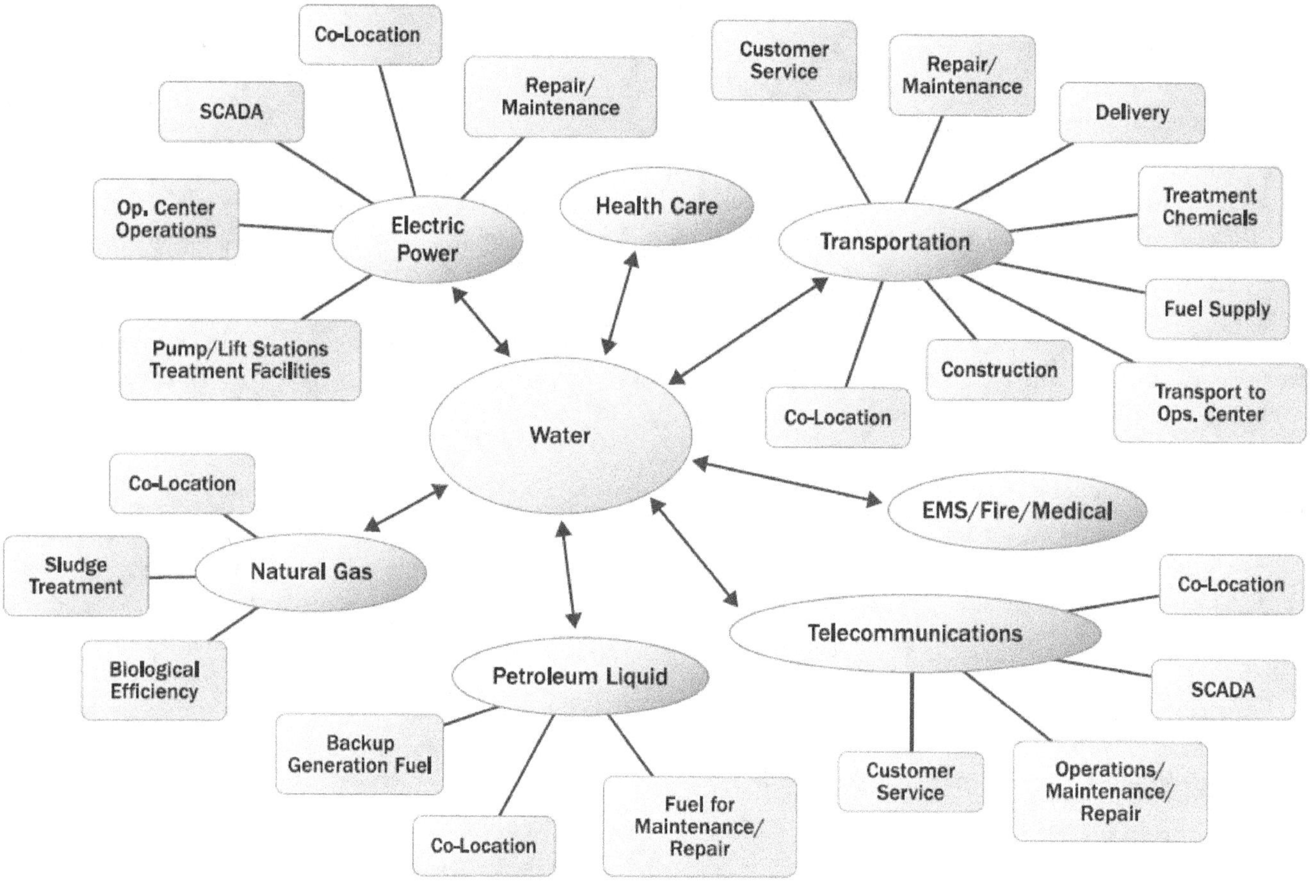

3.4 Assessing Vulnerabilities and Threats

Water Sector infrastructure is vulnerable to a variety of threats and hazards. The most plausible intentional attack methods (outsider and insider) facing the Water Sector, in no particular prioritized order, include improvised explosive devices; vehicle-borne improvised explosive devices; hazardous material releases; explosive devices in wastewater collection systems; chemical, biological, or radiological (CBR) contamination in drinking water distribution systems; assault; sabotage of water treatment systems; radiological dispersal devices; and cyber attacks on SCADA systems.

Natural disasters such as earthquakes, hurricanes, tornadoes, and floods also pose significant threats to the Water Sector; the sector has centuries of experience managing such risks. The Water Sector is conducting work related to the severity and frequency of earthquakes, hurricanes, tornadoes, and floods. This work will be incorporated into upgraded risk assessment methodologies; this is discussed in more detail below. Pandemic influenza is another hazard that threatens the continuity of Water Sector utility operations; vulnerabilities include unavailability of staff for daily operations and emergency response.

The Water Sector is also vulnerable to disruptions to other CIKR sectors given the interdependencies with other sectors. A disruption in many of the aforementioned interdependent sectors could have cascading effects on drinking water treatment and supply as well as wastewater collection and treatment.

3.5 Risk Assessment Initiatives

The Federal Government has worked with its partners on a number of products to better identify risk in the Water Sector. For example, EPA has created drinking water and wastewater threat documents to assist owners and operators in the conduct of risk assessments at the utility level. In 2006, DHS issued its Joint Strategic Water Sector Assessment. The intelligence community has worked with EPA to issue a number of classified reports on threats in the sector. On an annual basis EPA and its partners work with other SSAs on DHS's Strategic Homeland Infrastructure Risk Analysis; this report focuses on threat scenarios in the sector, resulting in a sector-specific and an overall national perspective on CIKR risk.

Many ongoing initiatives improve the security posture of the sector; specifically, risk assessment tools enable drinking water and wastewater utilities to identify, inventory, and assess the criticality of utility-specific components in much greater detail. The attributes that contribute to a utility's security may include components central to its mission and function that span the areas of the physical plant, personnel, knowledge base, information technology / SCADA, and customers.

Three risk assessment tools are widely used across the Water Sector: (1) Risk Assessment Methodology–Water (RAM–W); (2) Security and Environmental Management System (SEMS) emergency response checklist; and (3) Vulnerability Self-Assessment Tool (VSAT). Currently, DHS, EPA, and Water Sector partners are working collaboratively to ensure these existing assessment methodologies are upgraded and revised to provide Water Sector utility owners and operators with a consistent risk assessment approach that prioritizes utility investments and efforts to mitigate risk and tracks utility risk management performance and investment over time.

The ASME Innovative Technologies Institute and AWWA have developed a draft Risk Assessment Methodology Standard for Water and Wastewater Systems. Eventually this standard will provide a consistent and technically sound methodology to identify, analyze, quantify, and communicate the risks of specific terrorist attacks and natural hazards against critical water and wastewater systems and is consistent with the Risk Analysis and Management for Critical Asset Protection (RAMCAP™) framework.

To support more detailed risk assessment in the sector, partners are developing a consequence analysis tool, Water Health and Economic Analysis Tool (WHEAT), to assist in quantifying human health and economic consequences for a variety of asset-threat combinations that pose a risk in the sector. The tool will analyze three different event scenarios—drinking water distribution system contamination, release of a hazardous gas, and loss of operating assets. WHEAT will provide utilities with quantifiable estimates of public health and economic consequences to help create a more robust risk analysis for the sector.

AWWA has issued an American National Standards Institute (ANSI) standard, ANSI/AWWA G430: Security Practices for Operations and Management, which defines the minimum requirements for a protective security program for water or wastewater utilities that will promote the protection of employee safety, public health, public safety, and public confidence. This standard also encourages utilities to regularly review and update vulnerability assessments.

WERF, the WaterRF, DHS, and Idaho National Laboratory have developed a Control Systems Cybersecurity Self-Assessment Tool (CS2SAT) for use in the Water Sector to maximize the impact of cybersecurity self-awareness among the utilities. The CS2SAT tool is being integrated into Water Sector risk assessment tools and is cited continuously in the Cybersecurity Roadmap.

DHS released an updated cybersecurity assessment tool for the CIKR community; the Cyber Security Evaluation Tool (CSET) is a desktop software tool that guides users through a step-by-step process to evaluate their cyber systems and network security practices against recognized industry standards. Some of the benefits of CSET include: (1) contributing to an organization's risk management and decision-making process; (2) raising awareness and facilitating discussion on cybersecurity within the organization; (3) highlighting vulnerabilities in the organization's systems and providing recommendations on ways to address the vulnerability; (4) identifying areas of strength and best practices being followed in the organization; (5) providing a method to systematically compare and monitor improvement in the cyber systems; and (6) providing a common industry-wide tool for assessing cyber systems.

To further increase the security posture of the sector, a guide titled *Features of an Active and Effective Protective Program for Water and Wastewater Utilities* was developed to assist owners and operators in preventing, detecting, responding to, and recovering from the adverse effects of all hazards. These features originated as an outcome of a National Drinking Water Advisory Council workgroup in 2005. They have been updated to reflect the goals and objectives of the Water SSP, and describe the basic elements of a "protective program" for owners and operators of Water Sector utilities.

4. Prioritize Infrastructure

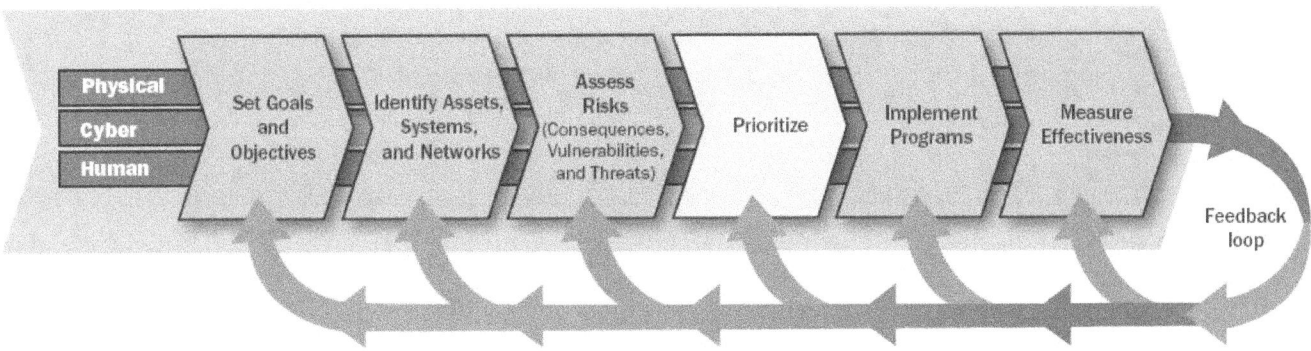

Continuous improvement to enhance protection of CIKR

This chapter describes the processes and criteria developed to better identify critical Water Sector assets across the country.

4.1 Component-level Prioritization within an Asset

Individual utility owners and operators are responsible for conducting risk assessments to identify the components of their utilities (e.g., pumps, generators, and SCADA systems) that are of higher consequence and concern in the event of an incident. Owners and operators have implicit screening processes to identify internal priorities related to business conditions, treatment, drinking water distribution, and reliability of wastewater collection to help them ensure continuity of operations. The importance of many components in a utility is highly variable and may depend on multiple considerations, including location and redundancy. Many of the Nation's Water Sector assets are built taking resilience into consideration; degrees of resilience vary from utility to utility across the country. The sector has well-developed protocols, organizations, and communication systems to ensure the reliability of service. Sector partners continue to work together to develop more informed threat, vulnerability, and consequence data to help utilities identify the most critical components of their systems.

4.2 Prioritizing Across Sector Assets

DHS's National Critical Infrastructure Prioritization Program identifies nationally significant critical assets and systems in order to enhance decision making related to CIKR protection. Under this program, assets designated as Level 1 and Level 2, if destroyed or disrupted, could cause some combination of significant casualties, major economic losses, or widespread and long-term disruption to national or regional well-being and governance capacity.

The Water Sector has developed its own criteria to better identify higher-consequence and higher-priority utilities nationwide. Utilities are placed in one of four levels, each representing a different grade of potential consequences. Four criteria are used to define Water Sector levels: (1) population served; (2) amount of chlorine gas stored on site; (3) economic impact; and (4) critical customers served. The sector uses EPA's SDWIS and PCS databases to assist in identifying these levels of assets and focus on public health and economic parameters that are directly linked to overall assessment of risk (vulnerability, consequence, and threat) in the sector.

Table 4-1 contains Water Sector level criteria for this voluntary risk management framework; a level determination is based on the highest single criterion threshold.

Table 4-1: Water Sector Level Criteria

Level Criteria	Level 1	Level 2	Level 3	Level 4
Drinking Water and Wastewater - Population Served (Drinking water only: retail plus wholesale)	≥ 1million	25,000 – 1 million	3,300 – 25,000	< 3,300
On-site Gaseous Chlorine Storage (average daily volume stored)	≥ 40 tons	20 – 40 tons	1 – 20 ton(s)	< 1 ton
Economic Impact (regional impact; not including value of statistical life)	≥ $100 billion	$5 – $100 billion	$100 million—$5 billion	< $100 million
Critical Customers Served	Federal Government Defined	Federal Government Defined	Two or more of the following: • Level 1 Trauma • Venue that holds 10,000 or more people • National Icons • Key Defense facilities • Key Defense Industrial Base assets	Not Applicable

The established structure to identify all Water Sector assets in correlation with the identification of nationally significant assets and the assessment of risk helps to improve the development of new and the modification of existing CIKR activities and initiatives. This process allows all partners to make more informed resource allocation decisions.

5. Develop and Implement Protection Initiatives and Resilience Strategies

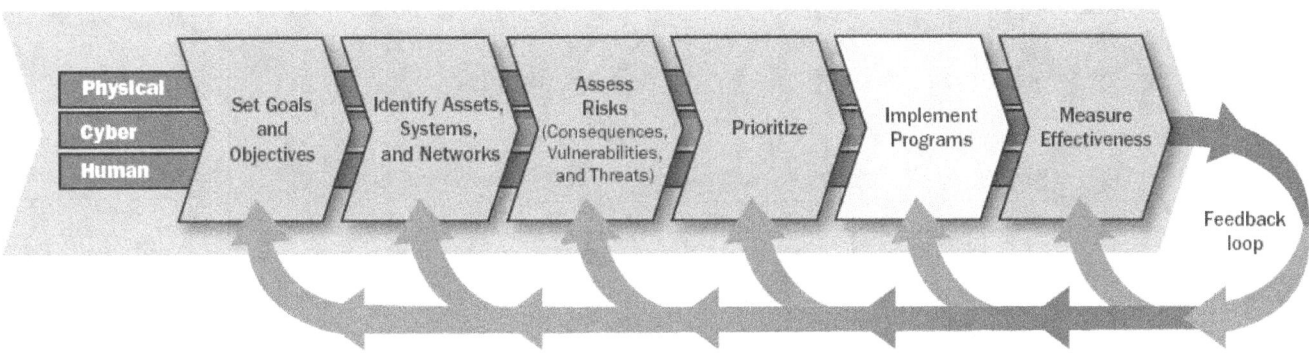

Continuous improvement to enhance protection of CIKR

This chapter includes information on the processes the Water Sector uses to develop and implement protection initiatives that are deployed throughout the sector. These processes guide infrastructure owners and operators on the most effective strategies for protecting their assets.

5.1 Overview and Determining the Need for Protection Initiatives and Resilience Strategies

Water Sector utilities have identified critical system components and have developed and installed countermeasures to fit the individual findings of conducted risk assessments. Countermeasures include improving staff awareness by providing relevant training; hardening assets and creating additional redundancies; and enhancing continuity of operations planning strategies, including the development of robust response and recovery capabilities.

Many system components, because of their distributed locations, their ease of access, or other reasons, do not lend themselves to hardening or cost-effective countermeasures. Preventing or detecting a manmade or naturally occurring event may not always be possible; therefore, improving a system's resilience improves continuity of operations by minimizing service disruptions. EPA and its Water Sector partners have developed holistic and integrated protection initiatives for all sector assets. EPA focuses on assets that service high-density populations (e.g., more than 100,000 people) because of the enhanced potential for greater consequences to public health, the environment, and local or regional economies.

The Water Sector has a long history of implementing initiatives to protect public health, the environment, and critical infrastructure. These initiatives support continuity of operations by mitigating threats, reducing vulnerabilities, and minimizing consequences, enabling more timely and efficient response and restoration after an event. A collaborative approach is used to determine and prioritize program needs. When a particular protection or resilience issue is identified, partners jointly analyze the issue, determine its importance, and recommend next steps, potentially including the implementation of protective programs and resilience strategies.

5.2 Characteristics of Protection Initiatives and Resilience Strategies

Water Sector protection initiatives and resilience strategies are aligned with the sector goals as described in chapter 1; these initiatives address the basic protection and resilience functions—prevention, detection, response, and recovery. Initial security efforts such as installing fencing, locks, and access systems focused more on the concepts of prevention and detection and less on response and recovery efforts. Now the logical progression within the sector has been toward building greater resilience through robust response and recovery efforts. Understanding interdependencies among water utilities and with other sectors is critical for guiding CIKR protection initiatives and resilience strategies. To that end, sector representatives continue to work with all partners to better understand and raise awareness of Water Sector interdependency issues as identified in chapter 3.

5.3 Summary of Protection Initiatives and Resilience Strategies

The Water Sector's goals and objectives provide the framework to develop and implement protective programs. EPA and sector partner organizations have all taken actions to support the sector's needs.

Owners and operators are responsible for implementing CIKR protection activities at the utility level, which allows protective programs to be tailored to the geography and conditions of that locality, with a focus on the higher-risk situations. Many water and wastewater utilities have conducted risk assessments and spent millions of dollars to reduce identified vulnerabilities and install protective measures. While various CIKR partners may take the lead on any one project, sector-wide collaboration, including the implementation of the NIPP partnership model, continues to provide enhanced communication through information and best practice sharing, resulting in opportunities to minimize duplication of efforts in program development and implementation. This collaborative approach continues to build public trust and confidence through strategic cost sharing-based initiatives.

To assist in meeting the Water SSP vision and goals, Water Sector partners have come together to develop the Strategic Roadmap, which is a living document that identifies the most pressing sector needs and prioritizes actions that industry and government can take to enhance water security and resilience. The document identifies three top-priority activities:

- **Priority 1 addresses the development of templates for detection, response, and recovery plans.** This endeavor aligns with sector goals 2 and 3 and will help utilities quickly and accurately determine the effectiveness and efficiency of their detection, response, and recovery plans and the need to take improvement actions;

  - **Description/Application:** Water utilities are confronted with an array of tools which can assist, or purport to assist, the utility in detecting, responding to, and recovering from an incident—whether a natural disaster or a human-induced event. Many utilities lack the resources to sift through these tools to identify the most relevant and useful applications. Also, some of these tools, though extremely informative, exist in a format and size that can pose a challenge for many utilities. Templates (e.g., checklists) that allow for tailoring such tools to a utility's unique conditions can provide decision makers with a way to assess risks, define costs, choose appropriate actions, and determine the effectiveness and efficiency of their plans. In the mid term (3-5 years), software tools, based on the templates, have the potential to automate and further simplify the utility's decision-making process as they continue to update and improve their plans.

- **Priority 2 focuses on updates to emergency response and recovery plans.** This activity aligns with the Water SSP goal 3 and will help utilities withstand and recover quickly from a catastrophic event by addressing current needs and incorporating lessons learned into ERPs; and

– **Description/Application:** In accordance with the *Features of an Active and Effective Program for Water and Wastewater Utilities,* emergency response and recovery plans should be updated on a regular basis to reflect changes in the understanding of risk, as defined in large part by new threats, vulnerabilities, and consequences. Periodic review and revision of emergency response and recovery plans can also identify weak and unworkable contingencies within the plan. Furthermore, this process can help utilities comply with National Incident Management System (NIMS) requirements and therefore qualify for protective program funds disbursed by DHS. Ongoing efforts by State drinking water primacy agencies can assist small drinking water utilities as they design, implement, and update their emergency response plans.

- **Priority 3 deals with increasing the public and political understanding of denial-of-service impacts and facilitates rate-based recovery of the cost of resilience and continuity initiatives.** This priority increases the funding available for a utility's security and resilience program by raising the understanding of the inherent value of water services among public officials, investors, and customers.

  – **Description/Application:** Today, the U.S. population benefits from a "hidden infrastructure" built with investments made over several decades. As a result, residents and public officials tend to undervalue water and wastewater services. Catastrophic events, such as hurricanes, ice storms, and earthquakes can impair, contaminate, or destroy critical infrastructure, with the costs of addressing such damage in many instances reaching the millions of dollars. Utilities often must seek the approval of public commissions or investors to fund new risk reduction efforts or to recover incurred emergency-related costs. Education and outreach activities that help utilities gain access to public officials and consumers and educate them on the real value of water and wastewater services—as well as the consequences of impaired or lost service—can overcome a general lack of awareness and garner support for both disaster and risk mitigation cost recovery. This effort can build on existing initiatives, such as those underway by State drinking water programs.

The Strategic Roadmap was finalized in October 2009 after several projects briefly described in Table 5-1 were initiated; more details on these projects can be found in appendix 5 of this document. Various Water Sector partners have undertaken these initiatives and while most align with the Strategic Roadmap, the Water SCC has not officially endorsed all of these projects. The initiatives are organized within the four sector goals; many align with the sector's priorities, and they also correspond to the Risk Mitigation Activities described in the *Water Sector Annual Report.* This report specifies the implementation status and progress of new and ongoing sector initiatives and the priorities that drive these efforts.

Table 5-1: CIKR Protection Initiatives

Goal 1: Sustain Protection of Public Health and the Environment
1. Water Security Initiative: Develops a contaminant warning system model for drinking water distribution systems.
2. Water Laboratory Alliance: Provides the drinking water sector an integrated nationwide network of laboratories with analytical capability and capacity to respond to intentional and unintentional drinking water contamination events.
3. Sector-Specific Metrics: Help Water Sector utilities assess their security and resilience capabilities.

Goal 2: Recognize and Reduce Risks in the Water Sector

4. Risk Assessment Methodologies: Build consistent vulnerability, consequence, and threat information into assessment methodologies that result in analysis and calculation of risk that is comparable within the sector.

5. WHEAT: Assists in better quantifying public health and economic impacts of a manmade or naturally occurring event.

6. Cybersecurity Roadmap: Provides a unified security strategy to help mitigate the risks associated with cyber systems.

7. Site Assistance Visits (SAVs) / Enhanced Critical Infrastructure Protection (ECIP) Visits: Help reduce vulnerabilities at high-consequence Water Sector utilities.

Goal 3: Maintain a Resilient Infrastructure

8. Emergency Response/Mutual Aid and Assistance Networks: Enhance preparedness and improve incident response by encouraging local utilities in every State to establish intrastate mutual aid and assistance agreements (e.g., WARNs).

9. Training and Exercises: Support continued development of tools and extensive training programs to help utilities enhance their emergency response preparedness and communicate with local first responders and public health providers during an incident response.

10. Business Continuity Planning (BCP): A risk management strategy or methodology that includes a variety of utility operation plans that may be specifically tailored to certain operating conditions but that collectively define or characterize how a utility will continue critical business functions during and after various incidents.

11. Community Case Study Pilot Project: Increases awareness of the benefits of implementing active and effective water preparedness programs.

12. Community-Based Water Resilience Initiative: Increases the overall preparedness of communities in the event of a water service interruption.

13. Decontamination Planning Strategies: Guide future decontamination activities for the sector that address a range of contamination scenarios related to the type of system, type of contaminant, type of media, type of incident, and extent of contamination.

14. Pandemic Planning: Provides tools and guidance to support Water Sector planning, preparedness, and response to pandemics, including the 2009 novel H1N1 virus.

15. Water Contaminant Information Tool (WCIT) and National Environmental Methods Index for Chemical, Biological, and Radiological (NEMI-CBR) Methods: Online tools that provide comprehensive data on possible water contaminants and analytical methods to assist eligible users in planning, detection, response, and recovery efforts.

Goal 4: Increase Communication, Outreach, and Public Confidence

16. WaterISAC: A tool for sharing sensitive information within the Water Sector.

The sector will continue regular communication among its partners, with DHS, and with other Federal agencies to ensure that protection initiatives are properly integrated into day-to-day utility operations. Sector partners are pursuing many initiatives jointly, which increases the likelihood that initiatives with the greatest potential are being pursued.

5.4 CIKR Protection Initiatives and Resilience Strategies Implementation and Monitoring

Implementation and maintenance of protection initiatives in the Water Sector is voluntary and generally occurs at the local utility level. EPA has encouraged implementation of protection initiatives by working with its partners to develop useful tools, training, technical assistance, guidance, and outreach and communication mechanisms that provide assistance to Water Sector assets to enhance their protection and resilience. These partnerships continue to provide significant educational tools and resources, in many cases at no cost to Water Sector partners, agencies, and authorities. All partners will continue to improve coordination and work together to ensure existing protection initiatives are consistently re-evaluated and these initiatives are properly implemented to successfully assist in meeting the Water SSP goals and objectives.

6. Measure Progress

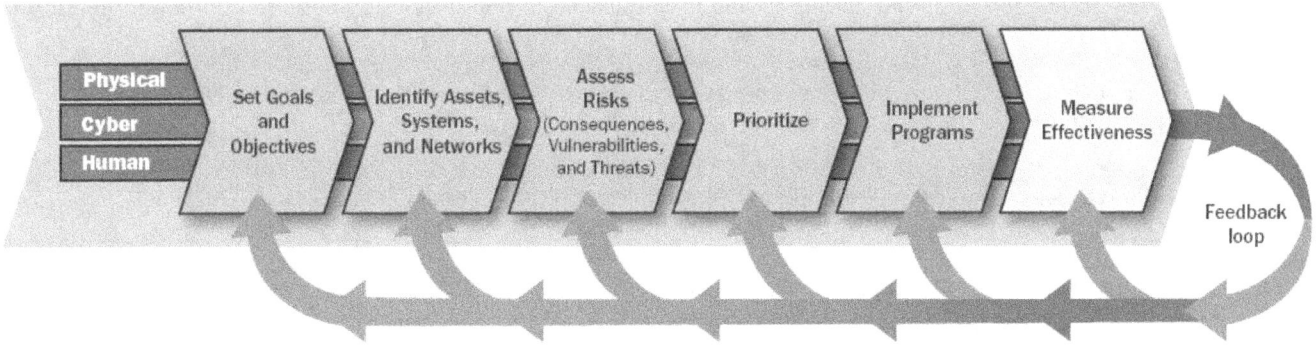

Continuous improvement to enhance protection of CIKR

Measuring progress is central to continuous improvement of the Water Sector protection program. The Water Sector developed sector-specific metrics and published in 2008 its first report, *Water Sector Measure Analysis*. Data analysis of the 2009 utility metrics collection is being conducted and will be published in the 2010 report. These measures allow for a more thorough evaluation of progress being made toward the goals and objectives set forth in the NIPP and the Water SSP. The sector-specific metrics are based on the goals, objectives, and supporting strategies outlined in the Water SSP and *Features of an Active and Effective Protective Program for Water and Wastewater Utilities*. The suite of metrics includes sixteen (16) utility activity metrics, fifteen (15) risk reduction metrics, three hazardous chemical security metrics, and seventeen (17) "other actor" metrics for Federal agencies, States, and associations. Additionally, EPA reports on Water Sector critical infrastructure initiatives through the sector annual reporting process established under HSPD-7.

6.1 Sector-Specific Activities, Information Collection, and Measuring Effectiveness

The WaterISAC acts as a third party and hosts a secure online reporting tool for utilities to report their metrics. The reporting tool uses a series of protocols governing how the collected data may be aggregated and reported nationally to other interested parties, including EPA and DHS. The data aggregation protocols are designed to ensure that the identity of individual utilities cannot be revealed. ASDWA manages the voluntary information-gathering initiative for State primacy agencies. State drinking water programs provide information designed to demonstrate individual State progress in improving the collective all-hazards security posture and to portray a sense of State engagement in activities that support the Water SSP. In 2009, State drinking water primacy agencies significantly expanded the scope of their metrics to better reflect the array of efforts and activities to support water security. ASIWPCA and EPA also collect "other actor" metrics.

The Water Sector has established the following principles for annual Water Sector-specific data collection that measures progress at the operational level: (1) participation in a national measurement program should be voluntary; (2) results of national aggregate measures should be presented only in aggregated form, and issues associated with the need for data confidentiality should be resolved before any national measurement program is put in place; (3) measures must help individual utilities better understand their own performance relative to the *Features of an Active and Effective Protective Program for Water and Wastewater Utilities*; (4) measures should be simple and focus on activities; over time, utilities should strive for measures of program achievement, outcomes, and performance; (5) strict comparability across utilities is not supportable for all measures at this time; (6) clear security policies, plans, and priorities are important precursors to effective measurement; (7) measures development and tracking should not compromise the security of a utility; (8) measurement baselines should not penalize proactive organizations; and (9) measurement information should be protected.

6.2 Sector-Specific Agency Reporting Requirements

HSPD-7 requires SSAs to provide DHS with annual reports that serve as a primary tool for assessing performance and reporting on progress in the sector. The Sector Annual Report accomplishes the following purposes: (1) provides a common vehicle across all sectors to communicate CIKR protection performance and progress to CIKR partners and other government entities; (2) establishes a baseline of existing sector-specific CIKR protection programs and initiatives; (3) identifies plans for SSA resource requirements and budget; (4) determines and explains how sector efforts support the national effort; (5) provides an overall progress report for the sector; (6) provides feedback to DHS, sectors, and other government entities to illustrate the continuous improvement of CIKR protection activities; and (7) helps identify and share beneficial practices from successful programs.

The Strategic Roadmap is a living document that identifies the most pressing sector needs and prioritizes actions that industry and government can take to enhance water security and resilience. Most needs identified in this Strategic Roadmap are addressed each year in the Water Sector Annual Report to DHS. Chapter 5 and appendix 5 of this document provide further information about sector initiatives that are included in the Water Sector Annual Report.

6.3 Using Metrics for Continuous Improvement

As traditional stewards of protecting public health and the environment, utility owners and operators have been very proactive in incorporating protection and emergency preparedness initiatives into their operating protocols to establish greater infrastructure resilience. Water Sector partners seek to assist utilities in overcoming the challenges owners and operators may face while trying to implement protective program strategies. EPA and its sector partners adapt protection efforts to account for progress achieved and changing threats, vulnerabilities, and consequences in the sector. To provide and protect information that pertains to the Water Sector's all-hazards security posture, the sector continues to identify and improve upon appropriate mechanisms for sharing sensitive information. Utilities take their responsibility to help protect the communities they serve seriously. While there is always room for improvement, results from the sector's first round of metrics collection clearly demonstrate an overwhelming commitment to continued security progress.

Results from the 2008 metrics initiative indicate that as a whole, drinking water and wastewater utilities have made significant progress in the areas of preparedness, awareness, and resilience. Specifically, ninety (90) percent of the two-hundred and ninety-seven (297) utilities responding to a sector-specific metrics data call indicated that they have integrated security and preparedness into their budgeting, training, and worker responsibilities; over ninety (90) percent are receiving validated security threat information; and over ninety (90) percent regularly review and update their ERPs. That utilities are voluntarily choosing to invest in these areas speaks volumes about the proactive nature of the sector.

The sector also regularly improves upon mechanisms for collecting, verifying, validating, storing, protecting, and tracking sector priorities and critical infrastructure information, but challenges still remain. Utility owners and operators lack confidence that the Federal Government can protect their asset vulnerability and consequence data; furthermore, the provisions of the Paperwork Reduction Act impact data collection efforts by Federal agencies.

The processes identified above for reporting on sector-specific metrics, as well as SSA requirements for reporting progress under HSPD-7 will continue; EPA and sector partners will focus on ways to continually improve the accuracy and usefulness of the information provided under these mechanisms.

7. CIKR Protection Research and Development

The Water Sector has a long history of investing in R&D initiatives to assist in setting public health standards and emergency response planning. This chapter includes information on Water Sector R&D priorities and initiatives.

7.1 Background

There are numerous R&D sector partners, including EPA, DHS S&T, States, WaterRF, WERF, water associations, educational institutions, national research laboratories, public and private research foundations, and other organizations. EPA's NHSRC conducts most Water Sector security R&D efforts; the NHSRC coordinates with all partners, creating a robust research agenda to promote safety, security, and resilience of utilities.

In 2003, EPA initially released the *Water Security Research and Technical Support Action Plan* (RAP), which identifies critical security issues for drinking water and wastewater, outlines research and technical support needs, and presents a prioritized list of research and technical support projects to address these needs. The process that created EPA's RAP involved a wide range of participants and included EPA staff; representatives of utilities; professional and industry associations; national laboratories; public advocacy groups; State water programs; water research organizations; vendors and contractors; the Bureau of Reclamation, Centers for Disease Control and Prevention (CDC), DHS, Food and Drug Administration (FDA), USACE, U.S. Geological Survey (USGS), National Institute of Occupational Safety and Health, National Institute of Standards and Technology, and National Science Foundation.

EPA met with the National Academy of Sciences (NAS) to obtain an independent peer assessment of its RAP. The NAS panel transmitted comments to EPA; these comments were reviewed by EPA and, where applicable, were incorporated into the draft RAP. The NAS then conducted a second review of the draft RAP. This review, along with additional inputs from co-sponsored EPA and WEF water security workshops, resulted in the RAP being updated and finalized in 2005.

The Agency also worked with WERF to identify needs and develop projects to improve wastewater security. WERF entered into a cooperative agreement with the Agency to address wastewater security-related activities. To advance this project further, WERF conducted a stakeholder wastewater security symposium. The needs and projects identified at the symposium are reflected in the RAP.

7.2 Collaboration

EPA, DHS, and Water Sector partners work together to identify R&D priorities. In 2008, the sector formed a R&D Working Group composed of GCC and Water SCC members to evaluate needs and make recommendations to EPA and DHS related to existing and new R&D initiatives.

EPA, as the Water SSA, represents the sector in the process that coordinates CIKR R&D across Federal agencies and with CIKR partners. That interagency process is managed by the Infrastructure Subcommittee (ISC), which is co-chaired by the White House Office of Science and Technology Policy (OSTP) and DHS S&T. The ISC, in conjunction with all SSAs, develops consensus and resolves issues related to R&D for infrastructure protection.

EPA is participating on the ISC support team that developed the National Critical Infrastructure Protection (NCIP) R&D Plan and is taking measures to ensure that these parallel efforts under HSPD-7 are coordinated within the Agency. The NCIP R&D Plan annual updates address R&D programs and requirements across Federal agencies, from CIKR owners and operators to international organizations such as the Global Water Research Coalition. The NCIP R&D Plan identifies technology themes that are common to many CIKR sectors, such as detection and sensor systems and analysis and decision support systems; resulting common technology solutions from these initiatives can potentially serve multiple sectors.

7.3 R&D Priorities

The RAP identifies seven Water Sector R&D priority topics. These priority topics support the four goals of the Water SSP and align with the themes outlined in the NCIP R&D Plan. Table 7-1 illustrates these relationships.

Table 7-1: Sector R&D Priority Topics Mapped to Sector Goals and the National CIKR R&D Themes

Water Sector R&D Priorities	Water Sector Goals	National CIKR R&D Themes
1. Protecting Drinking Water Systems from Physical and Cyber Threats	Goals 1 and 2	Protection and Prevention Systems
2. Identifying Drinking Water Threats, Contaminants, and Threat Scenarios	Goals 1 and 2	New and Emerging Threats and Vulnerabilities
3. Improving Analytical Methodologies and Monitoring Systems for Drinking Water	Goals 1, 2, and 3	Detection and Sensor Systems
4. Containing, Treating, Decontaminating, and Disposing of Contaminated Water and Materials	Goals 2 and 3	Protection and Prevention Systems
5. Planning for Contingencies and Addressing Infrastructure Interdependencies	Goal 3	Analysis and Decision Support Systems
6. Targeting Impacts on Human Health and Informing the Public about Risks	Goals 3 and 4	Human and Social Issues
7. Protecting Wastewater Treatment and Collection Systems	Goal 2	Protection and Prevention Systems

The sector uses these priorities to coordinate with DHS S&T in identifying R&D priorities each year. In particular the sector's R&D Working Group identifies capability gaps, such as the ability to quantify cascading consequences across sectors that motivate R&D projects. To prioritize the capability gaps, the R&D Working Group first decided on selection criteria, the most important of which were: (1) gaps should relate to identified risks; (2) they should provide user benefits; and (3) they should be possible to implement. Table 7-2 provides the resulting ranking of the capability gaps as determined by owners and operators, water associations, and government representatives.

Table 7-2: Water Sector Prioritized Capability Gaps

Water Sector Capability Gaps	Rank
Decontamination Research	1
Dependencies and Interdependencies	2
Risk Communications	3
Economic Impacts	4
Resilience and Recovery Time	5
Hydraulic Modeling	6
Monitoring and Response	7
Cybersecurity	8
Detection and Sensors (Chemical, Biological, Radiological)	9
Risk Assessment	10
Identification of High-Consequence Assets	11
Advanced Infrastructure Architecture and Design	12

Each of the R&D priorities listed above support the sector's protection and resilience goals.

7.4 R&D Management Processes

The extensive process that EPA used to create its RAP has established a baseline that facilitates annual updates of the Agency's portion of the NCIP R&D Plan. EPA continues to work with its partners to keep them apprised of any R&D efforts that could benefit the Water Sector; all partners monitor R&D progress, assess impact on the sector goals, and work together to update R&D strategies as needed.

EPA conducts ongoing internal analysis of threats and technologies to identify shortcomings, weaknesses, and additional needs, and will continue to develop its understanding of Water Sector vulnerabilities through analysis of physical and cyber systems and contaminant and threat scenarios. This effort improves and focuses the Agency's ability to address the sector's most pressing research needs. Finally, EPA staff continually surveys external research activities and reviews developments in water security technology by reading published papers, meeting individually with researchers, and attending and supporting conferences on water security. This process actively engages individuals and organizations that conduct R&D related to high-priority needs in protecting water infrastructure.

The transition process from R&D to implementing the technology for protection programs in the field is also critical to the success of R&D efforts. Each technology solution will require at least a slightly different implementation path. In most cases there will be a pilot project where the technology is implemented in the field prior to widespread use. EPA will work with sector partners to identify the best implementation process for a given technology.

8. Managing and Coordinating Sector-Specific Agency Responsibilities

EPA's responsibility as the SSA for the Water Sector involves: (1) collaborating and coordinating with all relevant Federal departments and agencies, State and local governments, and the private sector; (2) developing and upgrading risk assessment tools and training for the sector; and (3) encouraging risk management strategies to protect against and mitigate the effects of all-hazards events. This includes collaborating with sector partners and supporting sector coordinating mechanisms to: (1) identify, prioritize, and coordinate protection of CIKR; and (2) facilitate sharing of information on physical and cyber threats, vulnerabilities, incidents, potential protective measures, and best practices. Figure 8-1 represents the security-related relationships between EPA offices.

Figure 8-1: EPA Security-Related Organizational Chart

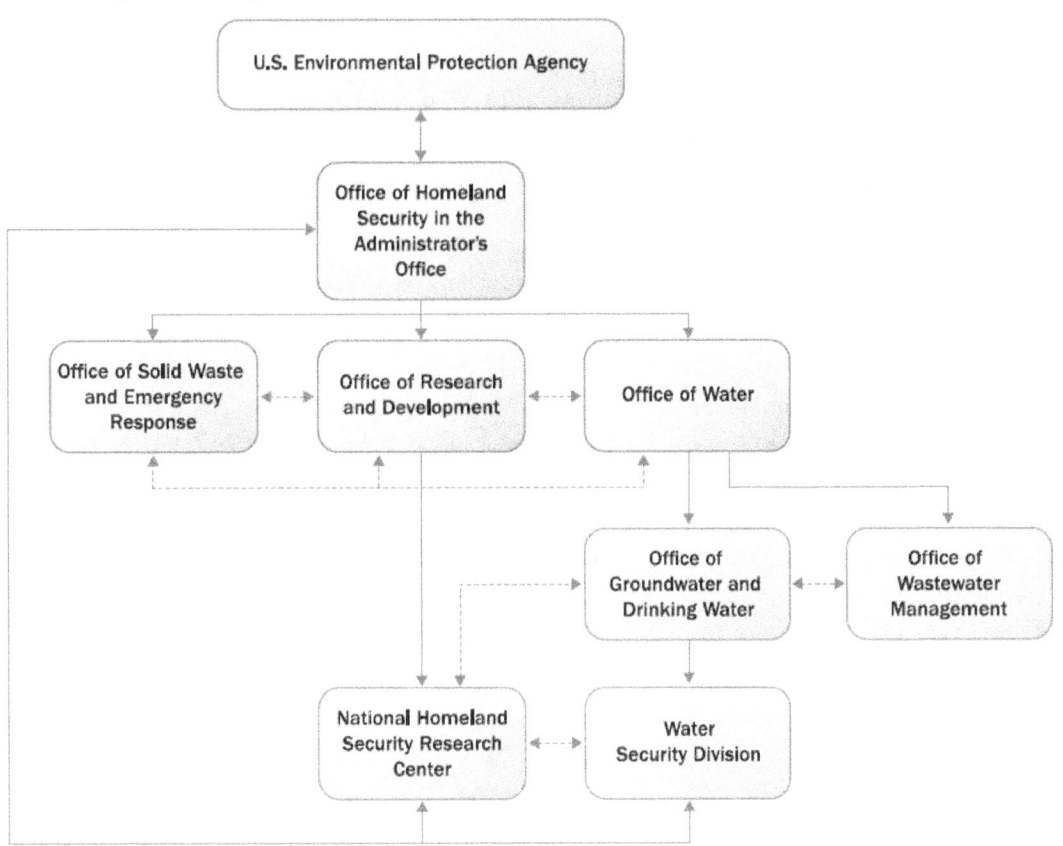

8.1 Program Management Approach

EPA has established organizational responsibilities to fulfill its role as the Water SSA. The Office of Homeland Security (OHS) is a component within the Office of the Administrator; the Water Security Division (WSD) is a component of the Office of Ground Water and Drinking Water in the Office of Water. The NHSRC is within the Office of Research and Development (ORD). Furthermore, the Office of Solid Waste and Emergency Response (OSWER), which has always dealt with emergency preparedness and response, expanded its mission to deal with homeland security-related activities.

The mission of OHS is to lead and coordinate homeland security activities and policy development across all EPA program areas, while ensuring consistent direction and facilitating effective communication of homeland security efforts both within and outside the Agency. OHS is charged by the Administrator with major areas of responsibility: (1) serving as the Agency-wide point of contact to the White House Homeland Security Council and DHS; (2) updating, facilitating, and tracking implementation of the EPA Homeland Security Strategy; (3) establishing a centralized and efficient system for receiving and evaluating important homeland security classified communications from multiple sources; (4) establishing IT systems that provide the latest information on Agency efforts on homeland security projects; and (5) supporting program offices and regional offices' ability to do "business as usual" while absorbing their new homeland security responsibilities.

WSD takes the lead for and aligns EPA Water Sector strategic planning and program management efforts. WSD's mission is to provide national leadership in developing and promoting security programs that enhance the sector's approach in preventing, detecting, responding to, and recovering from all hazards.

Although the WSD is structurally within the Office of Water, it is the lead for drinking water and wastewater infrastructure security; WSD works closely with EPA's Office of Wastewater Management on wastewater critical infrastructure matters.

NHSRC manages, coordinates, and supports various security-related R&D efforts. The Center provides reliable and responsive expertise and delivers products based on scientific research and technology evaluation in support of Water Sector goals.

OSWER is actively involved in counterterrorism planning and response efforts and continues to prepare for and will respond to terrorist threats from weapons of mass destruction (WMD) that have the capability to cause death or serious bodily injury to a significant number of people through release, dissemination, or impact of toxic poisonous chemicals; disease organisms; or radiation. Because of its inherent role in protecting human health and the environment from possible harmful effects of certain CBR materials, OSWER supports national homeland security-related efforts by: (1) helping State and local responders plan for emergencies; (2) coordinating with key Federal partners; (3) training first responders; and (4) providing resources in a man-made or naturally occurring incident.

All EPA offices continue to coordinate and collaborate to build on the Agency's robust all-hazards CIKR protection and resilience programs. WSD manages all SSA responsibilities for the Water Sector. NHSRC and WSD provide each other with the support and technical assistance needed to advance research-related security projects and programs that primarily impact the Water Sector (NHSRC research projects have influence on other sectors). OHS provides policy-oriented guidance and support to WSD, NHSRC, and OSWER.

In addition to having EPA Headquarters involved in Water Sector security, the Agency has ten regional offices across the country, each of which has a water security point of contact. Monthly coordination conference calls and activities occur between these points of contact and the EPA Headquarters offices. EPA maintains regular and frequent communication with its Water Sector partners (e.g., holding quarterly face-to-face meetings with all CIKR partner organizations, participating in SCC meetings, and leading GCC meetings). More details about sector partner relationships can be found in chapter 1 of this document.

8.2 Processing and Responsibilities

8.2.1 Water SSP Maintenance and Update

EPA, in concert with the Water SCC and GCC, is responsible for ensuring that the Water SSP is completed and updated based on significant events or changes in the sector's all-hazards approach to protecting CIKR and building additional resilience in the sector. The Water SSP is a strategic document that is collaboratively developed with the Water SCC and GCC by implementing the NIPP partnership model.

8.2.2 Water SSP Implementation Milestones

The Water SSP identifies overarching Water Sector critical infrastructure protection and resilience strategies which focus on all hazards, including but not limited to physical damage to infrastructure, contamination of drinking water, insider threats, cyber disruptions, cascading effects from other critical infrastructure, as well as natural disasters that could disable the infrastructure.

Critical infrastructure protection activity implementation and progress are captured in the *Water Sector Annual Report* that is developed in coordination with the Water SCC and GCC and then submitted to DHS every July. This report captures information regarding the implementation status of priority protective programs (milestones) and illustrates the continued progress of new and ongoing risk mitigation activities that are improving the security posture and increasing the resilience of the sector. Basic information on many sector risk mitigation activities can be found in chapter 5 and appendix 5 of the Water SSP.

8.2.3 Resources and Budgets

Given the variety of Federal, State, local, tribal, and public and private sector partners that contribute funds and other resources to protect the Water Sector, neither EPA nor any other entity has full authority over resources and budgets for the entire sector. While EPA can describe the Federal Water Sector contribution, it does not have a complete or accurate picture of the resources its sector partners are allocating; these non-SSA investments are substantial as described to the extent possible in section 8.2.3.2. EPA continues to work with its CIKR partners to provide information on available SSA resources and all groups coordinate to develop and share recommendations regarding allocation of sector resources and related funding. EPA's programmatic planning is based on the strategic approach outlined in chapter 5. Planning is guided by the goals outlined in this Water SSP and by analyzing the cost effectiveness and risk reduction aspects of protective programs that bring about increased resilience in the sector.

8.2.3.1 SSA Investments

EPA works closely with CIKR partners to promote the most efficient use of these Federal expenditures and offers its expertise to help the public and private utilities maximize the effectiveness of the resources allocated to support sector security, protection, resilience, and preparedness.

EPA, as the SSA for the Water Sector, supports homeland security initiatives in the Water Sector primarily through work in two programs, one in the Office of Water (OW) and the other in ORD. The Agency's annual budget request is submitted to the Office of Management and Budget (OMB) on the second Tuesday of each September. Between September and November, OW works with DHS and OMB to provide supporting documentation specific to EPA's request. Based on the initial submission and support documentation, OMB, coordinating with DHS, provides final decisions late in the calendar year regarding EPA's budget and resources available for sector security and related training. Relevant fiscal year budget information is provided in each *Water Sector Annual Report*.

8.2.3.2 Non-SSA Investments

Water Sector partners have responded with a significant investment through a variety of efforts at the national, State, and utility-specific levels. One of the most meaningful investments at the national level has been the amount of time provided by both national association staff members and utility volunteers for Water Sector protection and resilience-related activities. Examples include, but are not limited to, participating in the following: (1) Risk Assessment Methodology Working Group; (2) Sector-Specific Metrics Working Group; and (3) Threat Ensemble Vulnerability Assessment Working Group. Specific activities include: (1) attending partners meetings and regular Water SCC and GCC meetings; (2) providing comments for revisions to the NIPP, NIMS guidance, National Response Framework (NRF), and Water and Wastewater Sector Annex to the CIKR Pandemic Influenza Guidance; (3) assisting with the development of decontamination strategies; (4) leading the Cybersecurity Working Group in development of the Cybersecurity Roadmap; (5) promoting and assisting in the development of mutual aid and assistance networks for sharing of resources, including coordination with the Emergency Management Assistance Compact (EMAC); and (6) participating in the R&D Working Group to identify and prioritize capability gaps. The value of public and private sector partner investments of time and expense cannot be overstated.

Public sector investments span Federal, State, and local entities. DHS provides various funding and in-kind programs to support the Water Sector. Individual States have invested millions of dollars in training and oversight of protection and resilience-related issues. The States, through grant programs from DHS, have implemented Buffer Zone Protection Programs (BZPPs) and joint efforts to enhance response and recovery capabilities of communities across the United States. These efforts directly assist utilities in risk reduction and resilience building through consequence management activities. Also, some States have invested in utility-specific training for security awareness and have participated in DHS-led SAVs and ECIP visits.

Many of the national associations that represent drinking water utilities, wastewater utilities, and State drinking water and wastewater programs issue publications to support the sector. The National Environmental Training Center for Small Communities publishes E-Train Newsletter; WERF publishes Lateral; the Rural Community Assistance Partnership publishes Safe Drinking Water Trust eBulletin; ASDWA publishes Security Update; AMWA publishes Water Security Scan; AWWA publishes the Journal AWWA; and the NRWA publishes Rural Water Journal.

National Water Sector associations, State primacy agencies, and authorities at all levels have made significant commitments to supporting WARNs. Furthermore, meetings, conferences, and Webcasts of the national Water Sector associations regularly feature training, outreach, and education regarding security, emergency preparedness, and response.

At the local level, many Water Sector owners and operators have conducted and/or updated risk assessments and created or updated ERPs based on the findings of their risk assessments and have made significant monetary investments and time commitments to better protect their critical infrastructure and customers.

8.2.4 Training and Education

Successful implementation of all-hazards CIKR program initiatives relies on building and maintaining individual and organizational CIKR protection expertise. Training and education in a variety of areas is necessary to achieve and sustain this level of expertise. EPA operates a robust training program to provide specific instruction tailored to the size and type of a given Water Sector utility. EPA will continue with Water Sector partners to identify the most important topics for training (e.g., Incident Command System (ICS), NIMS, ERP, interdependencies) for utility owners and operators.

States have implemented locally customized training and exercise programs using their own tools as well as tools provided by EPA. Many of the exercises introduce State, local, and utility responders to the NRF and other response guidance; topic areas included water interdependencies, water supply system emergency response, and emergency planning drills.

8.3 Implementing the Sector Partnership Model

8.3.1 NIPP Coordinating Structures

The NIPP partnership model, illustrated in Figure 8-2, is the primary organizational structure for coordinating CIKR activities. SSAs are responsible for collaborating with public and private sector partners and encouraging development of appropriate information-sharing and analysis mechanisms within the sector. This includes coordination with State and local governments, as well as other Federal partners. EPA coordinates Water Sector protection and resilience efforts with the Water SCC (private sector owners and operators) and GCC (government sector partners), to seek input and direction and to identify gaps and next steps for CIKR protection and resilience activities within and across the sector. The NIPP partnership model encourages collaboration across sectors for both public and private sector partners through: (1) the Federal Senior Leadership Council (FSLC); (2) State, Local, Tribal and Territorial Government Coordinating Council (SLTTGCC); (3) RCCC; and (4) the CIKR Cross-Sector Council.

Figure 8-2: Sector Partnership Model

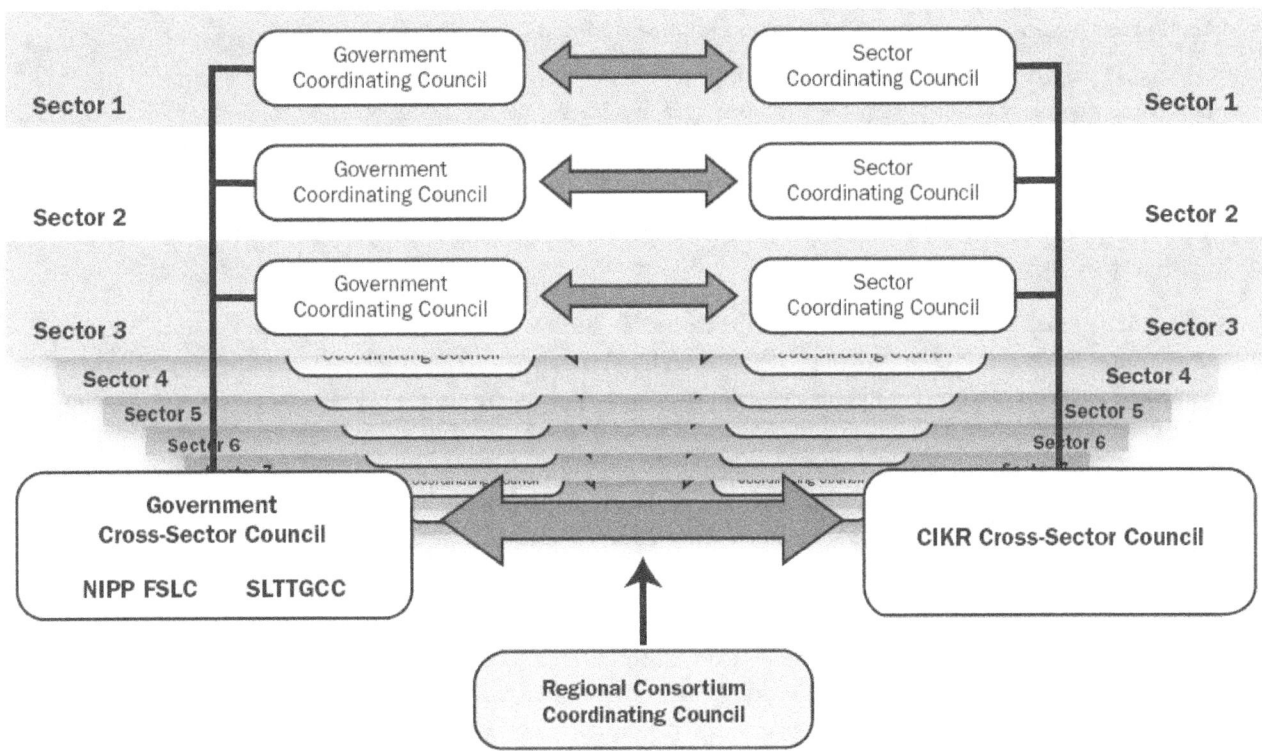

To assist in further coordination, CIPAC provides a legal framework for members of the SCCs and GCCs to engage in joint CIKR protection-related activities. The Chairman of either the Water SCC or GCC can facilitate and organize joint council meetings in consultation with the chairman of the other council. CIPAC serves as a forum for government and private sector partners to engage in a broad spectrum of activities, such as planning, coordination, implementation, and operational issues. The Water Sector has used and benefited from this framework and has formed a number of working groups under CIPAC, such as the Metrics Working Group, Decontamination Working Group, Cyber Security Working Group, R&D Working Group, Emergency Response Working Group, Risk Assessment Working Group, and Sector Strategic Planning Working Group.

8.3.2 State, Regional, Local, Tribal, and Territorial Government Entities

EPA depends heavily on State drinking water primacy agencies and the wastewater permitting authorities that implement the SDWA and CWA. Because almost all drinking water and wastewater programs are delegated to the States, EPA works with the States to ensure implementation of programmatic and security-related initiatives. State programs maintain inventories of drinking water and wastewater facilities, regularly inspect these systems, provide technical assistance, maintain laboratory and operator certification programs, and monitor compliance by reviewing analytical results. States review and approve plans and specifications for new and expanded facilities and they take enforcement actions as needed.

EPA coordinates its protection and resilience efforts with State and local entities that represent the Water Sector. This coordination includes facilitating meetings, seeking input on sector security concerns and issues, and raising security awareness. Many of these entities are channels to provide information and training opportunities to utilities. Two of the main State-related organizations that EPA works with are ASDWA and ASIWPCA, which represent drinking water and wastewater programs in the States, the District of Columbia, Territories, and commonwealths across the country.

8.3.3 Academia, Research Centers, Think Tanks, and International Coordination

The Water Sector established working relationships with a number of research organizations such as the WaterRF and WERF. These entities and others conduct research, identify gaps, and develop security-related tools and products. The academic and research center communities play important roles in enabling national CIKR protection and implementation of the NIPP. International coordination and identification of assets is addressed in section 1.2.6.

8.4 Information Sharing and Protection

The dissemination of important and relevant security information, such as physical and cyber threats, vulnerabilities, incidents, protective measures, and best practices, among Federal, State, local, tribal, and territorial governments is a critical component of protection and resilience. While the GCC and Water SCC framework is an effective way for sector partners to communicate and coordinate efforts, there are additional mechanisms that foster good communication and information sharing. Chapters 4, 5, and 6 identify information-sharing mechanisms currently in place among CIKR partners. Water Sector partners are responsible for collaborating to improve information sharing and tools. Through Web sites, partner updates, e-mail trees, Web-casts, and other mechanisms, the sector is able to share unclassified security-related information.

WaterISAC

The WaterISAC receives secure classified information relevant to protection of the sector. WaterISAC is a secure, Internet-based, rapid notification system and information resource for gathering, evaluating, and sharing unclassified, but sensitive security-related information on drinking water and wastewater systems in support of utility executives, managers, operators, and security officers.

WaterISAC provides a unique link between Water Sector partners and environmental, homeland security, law enforcement, intelligence, and public health agencies. It offers communication and information tools such as public bulletins and advisories for both national and specific security alerts for the sector. Subscribers to WaterISAC are quickly notified of the latest government alerts on water security and receive expert analysis about how a reported threat may impact their water system.

Operations are routinely coordinated with DHS and EPA as they pertain to data sharing, correlation, and safeguarding with the goal of achieving cooperative analysis to identify and effectively respond to threats to the Water Sector. WaterISAC continues to improve upon methods of receiving information from utilities through its secure, online reporting mechanism, while simultaneously coordinating and sharing information with its large subscriber base and continues to hold intelligence analyst meetings to review threat levels on at least a quarterly basis.

There are over 11,000 WaterISAC subscribers; working in conjunction with EPA, trial subscriptions to WaterISAC are being offered to drinking and wastewater utilities around the country. WaterISAC is also exploring options to offer NIMS training for water and wastewater utility personnel through Web-based means and now has staff access to the National Incident Command Center, has solidified its contacts within the information-sharing and intelligence communities, and continues to serve as the official communications and operational arm of the Water SCC.

Threat Information Sharing

DHS, coordinating with the FBI and other U.S. Intelligence Community elements, is responsible for sharing critical infrastructure threat-related information with sector partners. EPA, as the Water SSA, where and when appropriate, assists DHS in sharing this type of information. In performing this role, EPA acknowledges that WaterISAC has a designated role as the official communications and operational arm of the Water Sector. To help the sector better understand its threats, DHS, FBI, and EPA have provided a classified threat briefing to those with clearances on the Water SCC and GCC.

Information sharing and communications are vital to CIKR activities; challenges still exist with expanding and sharing both sensitive and non-sensitive information. Water Sector partners recognize the need to continue to improve information-sharing capabilities that are explicitly linked to critical infrastructure resilience goals and governance. Science-based modeling, simulation, and analysis studies might be used to establish better communication mechanisms and could provide the groundwork for educational materials to all sector partners. The path forward involves a wide array of activities that will align with the priorities and goals set in the Water SSP and will forge strong relationships between Water Sector utility owners and operators, DHS, and Federal, State, and local law enforcement to increase communication and enhance the sharing of threat and security information.

Appendix 1: List of Acronyms and Abbreviations

AMWA	Association of Metropolitan Water Agencies
ANSI	American National Standards Institute
APHL	Association of Public Health Laboratories
ASDWA	Association of State Drinking Water Administrators
ASIWPCA	Association of State and Interstate Water Pollution Control Administrators
AWWA	American Water Works Association
BCP	Business Continuity Planning
BLM	Bureau of Land Management
BZPP	Buffer Zone Protection Program
CBR	Chemical, Biological, or Radiological
CDC	Centers for Disease Control and Prevention
CFR	Code of Federal Regulations
CIKR	Critical Infrastructure and Key Resources
CIPAC	Critical Infrastructure Partnership Advisory Council
CRWU	Climate Ready Water Utilities
CS2SAT	Control Systems Cybersecurity Self–Assessment Tool
CSET	Cyber Security Evaluation Tool
CWA	Clean Water Act
CWS	Community Water System
DHS	U.S. Department of Homeland Security
DoD	U.S. Department of Defense
DOE	U.S. Department of Energy
DOI	U.S. Department of the Interior
DOS	U.S. Department of State
DOT	U.S. Department of Transportation

DSRC	Distribution System Research Consortium
ECIP	Enhanced Critical Infrastructure Protection
EMAC	Emergency Management Assistance Compact
EPA	U.S. Environmental Protection Agency
ERP	Emergency Response Plan
FBI	Federal Bureau of Investigation
FDA	U.S. Food and Drug Administration
FSLC	Federal Senior Leadership Council
GAO	U.S. Government Accountability Office
GCC	Government Coordinating Council
HHS	U.S. Department of Health and Human Services
HSPD	Homeland Security Presidential Directive
ICS	Incident Command System
IP	Office of Infrastructure Protection
ISC	Infrastructure Subcommittee
LRN	Laboratory Response Network
MGD	Million Gallons per Day
NACWA	National Association of Clean Water Agencies
NAS	National Academy of Sciences
NAWC	National Association of Water Companies
NCIP	National Critical Infrastructure Protection
NEMI-CBR	National Environmental Methods Index—Chemical, Biological, and Radiological
NFPA	National Fire Protection Administration
NGA	National Governors Association
NHSRC	National Homeland Security Research Center
NIMS	National Incident Management System
NIPP	National Infrastructure Protection Plan
NPDES	National Pollutant Discharge Elimination System
NPS	National Park Service
NRF	National Response Framework
NRWA	National Rural Water Association
NTNCWS	Non-Transient Non-Community Water System
OCA	Offsite Consequence Analysis
OHS	Office of Homeland Security
OMB	Office of Management and Budget

ORD	Office of Research and Development
OSTP	Office of Science and Technology Policy
OSWER	Office of Solid Waste and Emergency Response
OW	Office of Water
PCS	Permit Compliance System
POTW	Publicly Owned Treatment Works
PSA	Protective Security Advisor
PWS	Public Water System
R&D	Research and Development
RAMCAP™	Risk Analysis and Management for Critical Asset Protection
RAM–W	Risk Assessment Methodology–Water
RCCC	Regional Consortium Coordinating Council
RMP	Risk Management Plan
S&T	Science and Technology Directorate
SAV	Site Assistance Visit
SCADA	Supervisory Control and Data Acquisition
SCC	Sector Coordinating Council
SDWA	Safe Drinking Water Act
SDWIS	Safe Drinking Water Information System
SEMS	Security and Environmental Management System
SLTTGCC	State, Local, Tribal, and Territorial Government Coordinating Council
SSA	Sector-Specific Agency
SSP	Sector-Specific Plan
TNCWS	Transient Non-Community Water System
U.S.C.	United States Code
USACE	U.S. Army Corps of Engineers
USDA	U.S. Department of Agriculture
USGS	U.S. Geological Survey
VSAT	Vulnerability Self-Assessment Tool
WARN	Water and Wastewater Agency Response Network
Water SCC	Water Sector Coordinating Council
WaterISAC	Water Information Sharing and Analysis Center
WaterRF	Water Research Foundation
Water SSP	Water Sector-Specific Plan
WCIT	Water Contaminant Information Tool

WEF	Water Environment Federation
WERF	Water Environment Research Foundation
WHEAT	Water Health and Economic Analysis Tool
WMD	Weapons of Mass Destruction
WSD	Water Security Division

Appendix 2: Authorities

This appendix breaks out pertinent authorities that impact the Water Sector into several broad categories: (1) presidential directives; (2) general homeland security laws; and (3) a number of environmental laws.

A2.1 Homeland Security Presidential Directive 7 (critical infrastructure identification, prioritization, and protection, December 17, 2003)

HSPD-7 establishes a national policy for Federal departments and agencies to identify and prioritize national CIKR to protect them from terrorist attacks that could: (1) cause catastrophic health effects or mass casualties comparable to WMD; (2) impair the ability of Federal departments and agencies to perform essential missions or ensure protection of public health and safety; (3) undermine State and local government capacities to maintain order and deliver minimum essential public services; (4) damage the Water Sector's capability to ensure the orderly functioning of the economy and delivery of essential services; (5) have a negative impact on the economy through the cascading disruption of other CIKR; and (6) undermine public morale and confidence in our national economic and political institutions.

The Secretary of Homeland Security is tasked with integrating and coordinating implementation efforts among Federal departments and agencies, State and local governments, and the private sector. The Secretary is to establish uniform policies, approaches, guidelines, and methodologies for integrating critical infrastructure and risk management activities within and across sectors, and for developing metrics as part of a national CIKR protection plan. The Secretary also maintains an organization to serve as a focal point for cybersecurity, and prepares an annual Federal R&D plan. Federal agencies are required to work with State and local governments and the Water Sector to accomplish these objectives, and are instructed to appropriately protect information associated with carrying out this directive. The directive focuses on CIKR that, if exploited, could cause catastrophic health impacts or mass casualties and identifies EPA as the SSA for the Water Sector, known as the Drinking Water and Water Treatment Sector in this directive. HSPD-7 calls on SSAs to: (1) collaborate with Federal departments and agencies, State and local governments, and the private sector, and conduct or facilitate vulnerability assessments of the sector; (2) encourage risk management strategies to protect against and mitigate the effects of an attack; and (3) promote continued development of information-sharing and analysis mechanisms.

A2.2 Homeland Security Presidential Directive 8 (national preparedness, December 17, 2003)

HSPD-8 establishes policies to strengthen U.S. ability to prevent and respond to threatened or actual domestic terrorist attacks, major disasters, and other emergencies through development of a national, domestic all-hazards preparedness goal. It provides for State grants to build—through planning, training, and exercises—the capacity of first responders to react to terrorist events.

Funds also can be used to purchase equipment. States are required to develop State-specific plans. The directive also calls for development of quantifiable performance measures.

A2.3 Homeland Security Presidential Directive 9 (defense of United States agriculture and food, January 30, 2004)

HSPD-9 establishes a national policy to defend the water, agriculture, and food system against terrorist attacks, major disasters, and other emergencies. It calls on EPA and other Federal agencies to: (1) build upon and expand current monitoring and surveillance programs for public health and water quality that provide early detection and awareness of disease, pest, or poisonous agents; (2) develop nationwide laboratory networks for water quality that integrate existing Federal and State laboratory resources; (3) develop and enhance intelligence capabilities to include collection and analysis of information concerning threats, delivery systems, and methods that could be directed against the Water Sector; and (4) accelerate and expand countermeasure R&D of detection methods, prevention technologies, agent characterization, and dose-response relationships for high-consequence agents.

A2.4 Homeland Security Presidential Directive 10 (biodefense for the 21st century, April 24, 2004)

HSPD-10 provides a comprehensive framework for the Nation's biodefense. It builds on past accomplishments, specifies roles and responsibilities, and integrates the work of various communities—national security, medical, public health, intelligence, diplomatic, agricultural, and law enforcement—into a sustained and focused national effort against biological weapons threats. The directive focuses on threat awareness, prevention and protection, surveillance and detection, and response and recovery. Specific direction to departments and agencies to carry out this biodefense program is contained in a classified document.

A2.5 Safe Drinking Water Act, 42 United States Code (U.S.C.) 300F-300J-26

The general provisions of the SDWA, established in 1974, provide a basis for drinking water security by protecting water quality and underground sources of drinking water. To protect the quality of public drinking water, EPA established regulations for national primary and secondary drinking water standards. Forty-nine of the 50 States have received primacy from EPA to administer the drinking water program. To obtain primacy, States must adopt regulations no less stringent than the Federal Government's and must meet other conditions. Pertinent conditions include enforcement authority; the ability to conduct sanitary survey inspections of water utilities; and requirements to certify and approve laboratories for sample analysis, maintain an inventory of PWSs (utilities) in the State, and have an adequate plan to provide for safe drinking water during emergencies.

The statute applies to PWSs—systems for provision of water to the public for human consumption through pipes and other constructed conveyances, including such Federal facilities as military bases and hospitals, and other sites with their own drinking water systems. Drinking water programs most applicable to water security include wellhead protection and source water protection, protection of underground sources of drinking water, sanitary survey inspections, maintenance of records, and water quality monitoring.

A2.6 Public Health Security and Bioterrorism Preparedness and Response Act of 2002 (Bioterrorism Act), Public Law 107-188

Among other provisions, the Bioterrorism Act amends the SDWA by inserting Title IV, Drinking Water Security and Safety, into Title XIV of the Public Health Services Act as sections 1433, 1434, and 1435. Initiatives and accomplishments under the act are as follows: (1) EPA provided the baseline probable threat information required to complete vulnerability assessments; (2) on or before December 31, 2004, each CWS serving more than 3,300 persons conducted a vulnerability assessment, certified its completion, and submitted a copy to EPA; (3) each CWS serving more than 3,300 persons prepared or revised an ERP that incorporated the vulnerability assessment findings, and certified to EPA that the system had completed such a plan within 6 months of completing an assessment; (4) EPA developed a protocol to protect this information; (5) EPA developed vulnerability assessment guidance for systems serving 3,300 or fewer persons; and (6) EPA conducted research studies in prevention, detection, and response to intentional introduction of contaminants into CWSs and their source water; methods and means by which terrorists could disrupt the supply of safe drinking water or act against drinking water infrastructure; and methods and means by which alternative supplies of drinking water could be provided in the event of destruction, impairment, or contamination of CWSs.

It is important to note that the term "vulnerability assessment" is interchangeable with the term "risk assessment" in the Water Sector due to the language of the Bioterrorism Act. Water Sector vulnerability assessments are equivalent to risk assessments since the methodologies developed for the Water Sector consider all the components of risk (threat, vulnerability, and consequence).

A2.7 Federal Water Pollution Control Act (Clean Water Act), 33 U.S.C. 1251-1387

The CWA governs the quality of discharges to surface and groundwater. It establishes national, technology-based standards for municipal waste treatment and numerous categories of industrial point-source discharges (e.g., discharges from such fixed sources as pipes and ditches); requires States, and in some cases tribes, to enact and implement water quality standards to attain designated water-body uses; addresses water pollutants; and regulates dredge-and-fill activities and wetlands. The Act provides a number of enforcement authorities for EPA and States that have accepted permitting authority. It also applies these requirements to such Federal facilities as military installations and Department of Energy (DOE) sites. Provisions most applicable to security include the prohibition of discharges into waters of the United States, development of pretreatment effluent standards, oil and hazardous substance liability, and imminent and substantial endangerment authorities.

A2.8 Clean Air Act, Section 112(r), 42 U.S.C. 7401-7671q, EPA Risk Management Plan Regulation (40 Code of Federal Regulations (CFR) Part 68)

Under the authority of section 112(r) of the Clean Air Act, the Chemical Accident Prevention Provisions require facilities that produce, handle, process, distribute, or store certain chemicals in certain threshold amounts (e.g., 2,500 pounds of chlorine) to develop a Risk Management Program, prepare a Risk Management Plan (RMP), and submit the RMP to EPA. Covered facilities were initially required to comply with the rule in 1999, and the rule has been amended on several occasions since 1999, most recently in 2004. The RMP must include an executive summary that provides a brief description of the facility's accidental release prevention and emergency response policies, the regulated substances handled at the facility, the worst-case release scenario(s) and alternative release scenario(s), the five-year accident history of the facility, the ERP, and planned changes to improve safety at the facility (see 40 CFR Part 68). The full RMP also includes an Offsite Consequences Analysis (OCA), which provides the estimated extent of a worst-case scenario.

Pursuant to the Chemical Safety Information, Site Security and Fuels Regulatory Relief Act (Public Law 106-40), OCA information is no longer made available to the public via the EPA website. However, under the law, Federal reading rooms provide the public with read-only access to paper copies of RMPs, including OCA information submitted by chemical facilities. Other chemicals that may be present at Water Sector utilities, including ammonia, sulfur dioxide, and chlorine dioxide, also trigger RMP regulatory requirements if they exceed certain threshold quantities.

Appendix 3: Water Sector CIKR Partners

A3.1 Other Pertinent Sectors

Chemical Sector. DHS IP is the SSA for the Chemical Sector. EPA coordinates with this office regarding risks associated with the storage, transport, and use of chemicals in water utility operations. Water Sector owners and operators coordinate with Federal, State, and local authorities to ensure compliance with chemical safety regulations.

Dams Sector. Dams and reservoirs provide water for a large fraction of the population. EPA coordinates with dam owners and operators, including DOI, which have responsibility for managing the Nation's dams and reservoirs, including pumping plants, canals, and pipelines.

Emergency Services Sector. DHS IP is the SSA for the Emergency Services Sector. EPA coordinates with this sector regarding provision of water for emergency response. At the operational level, water utilities ensure that emergency responders have sufficient information to respond effectively to incidents at their facilities.

Energy Sector. DOE is the SSA for the Energy Sector. The primary interdependency with the Energy Sector is the need for a stable and reliable source of energy to power water and wastewater utilities. EPA works closely with several DOE national laboratories, including Argonne, Lawrence Livermore, Los Alamos, and Sandia. These laboratories are represented on EPA's Distribution System Research Consortium (DSRC). The Agency worked with the Sandia laboratory, along with WaterRF to develop a drinking water risk assessment tool that is used primarily by large drinking water systems to evaluate their threats, vulnerabilities, and consequences. The products of these efforts are tools and guidance for drinking water and wastewater utilities to minimize the likelihood that critical services will be disrupted as a result of cascading and escalating effects of either manmade or natural events. EPA also coordinates with the Federal Energy Regulatory Commission (FERC), which regulates interstate transmission of natural gas, oil, and electricity. EPA's interactions with FERC primarily involve the Water Sector's interdependency with electric power.

Food and Agriculture Sector & Healthcare and Public Health Sector. USDA's Rural Utilities Service provides funding and support for rural America, including small, rural drinking water and wastewater utilities. USDA's Forest Service provides source-water protection initiatives concerning sources of drinking water that are located in or originate on Forest Service lands. The service also operates water utilities (e.g., campgrounds, picnic grounds, and some ranger stations), and there are some CWS sources on National Forest land. With issuance of HSPD-9, USDA expanded its role with the EPA to build upon and increase current monitoring and surveillance programs that provide early detection and awareness of disease, pest, and poisonous agents.

Several agencies within HHS, including the CDC, FDA, and Indian Health Service have worked closely with EPA. In particular, CDC and FDA played important roles in helping define biological, chemical, and radiological threats to drinking water. EPA will establish a memorandum of agreement with CDC to leverage resources in the Laboratory Response Network (LRN), which includes private, State, and government laboratories and can mobilize quickly to test for possible terror-related contaminants.

The agreement will acknowledge that significant national laboratory testing capacity derives from use of established laboratory networks such as the LRN, Food Emergency Response Network, National Animal Health Laboratory Network, National Plant Diagnostic Network, and Federal agencies with responsibility and authority for laboratory preparedness and response (collectively referred to as the Networks) and the Environmental Response Laboratory Network. The agreement respects existing relationships, policies, and operating procedures of the Networks or any similar group of laboratories with relationships involving Federal funding, direction, or other cooperative arrangements.

Under EPA's Water Security Initiative, drinking water contamination warning system pilots are being established in various cities and LRN laboratories are providing critical sample analysis capability and capacity for these pilots. For example, a letter of intent between EPA and an LRN laboratory operated by the Ohio Department of Health enabled the analysis of samples from a drinking water contamination warning system pilot in Cincinnati using the LRN biological threat agent screening protocol and made available the necessary LRN reagents for this analysis.

CDC counterparts are members of EPA's NHSRC DSRC, and FDA regulates bottled drinking water, which may be used as a short-term remedy when PWS service is interrupted. FDA is required to regulate bottled water to standards at least as stringent as those issued by EPA under the SDWA. The Water Sector also shares interdependencies with HHS regarding interstate conveyance carriers (e.g., planes and trains with potable water on board); EPA will establish a memorandum of understanding with FDA to deal with these carriers.

Information Technology Sector. DHS National Cybersecurity Division (NCSD) is the SSA for the Information Technology Sector. NCSD oversees the protection of IT industry, and also has a cross-sector responsibility regarding the security of industrial control systems that are critical for all sector operations. NCSD provides cybersecurity threat and vulnerability information to benefit EPA and all SSAs.

Transportation Systems Sector. The Department of Transportation (DOT) is responsible for promoting the safety, efficiency, effectiveness, and economic well being of the Nation's transportation systems. The Water Sector shares several key interdependencies with DOT, including its reliance on the Transportation Systems Sector to provide chemicals, such as gaseous chlorine, and supplies for drinking water and wastewater treatment facilities. Highways and railways can also present vulnerabilities to the Water Sector where they pass near or over sources of drinking water.

A3.2 CIKR Associations and Partners

Association of Metropolitan Water Agencies represents the largest publicly owned drinking water systems in the United States. Collectively, member agencies serve 130 million people. AMWA oversees the WaterISAC, which serves as the operational and communications arm of the sector. WaterISAC is a centralized resource that gathers, analyzes, and disseminates Water Sector centric all-hazards security information. It serves drinking water and wastewater utilities of all sizes and ownership types. It has the most comprehensive and readily available online library that includes contaminant databases and resources about Water Sector vulnerabilities, incidents, and solutions for all hazards.

Association of Public Health Laboratories (APHL) represents the Nation's public health and environmental laboratories. In an effort to strengthen the Nation's laboratory capability and capacity, EPA and APHL have formed a partnership to formulate sound public health and environmental policies, offer training and education, and improve overall laboratory management and practices nationwide.

Association of State and Interstate Water Pollution Control Administrators is a national, nonpartisan professional organization. Members are State, Interstate and Territorial officials who are responsible for the implementation of surface water protection programs throughout the Nation. ASIWPCA serves as the national voice for State clean water program concerns and policies, and facilitates their communication with the Federal Government. Through sound policy and education, ASIWPCA strives to protect and restore watersheds to achieve clean water for everyone.

Association of State Drinking Water Administrators represents drinking water agencies in the 50 States, Territories, the Navajo Nation, and the District of Columbia. ASDWA's purpose includes supporting States in their efforts to protect public health through the assurance of high quality drinking water, encouraging the interchange of experience among State drinking water programs, and promoting responsible, reasonable, and feasible drinking water programs at the State and Federal levels. ASDWA also provides advice, counsel, and expertise to organizations and entities involved in drinking water, including Congress and the EPA.

American Water Works Association represents water utilities of all sizes and ownership types. Its 60,000-plus members represent the full spectrum of the drinking water community, including treatment plant operators and managers, scientists, environmentalists, manufacturers, academics, engineers, and regulators. Membership includes more than 4,600 utilities that supply water to 180 million North Americans.

International City/County Management Association is a professional and educational organization composed of 9,000 chief appointed managers, administrators, and assistants in cities, towns, counties, and regional entities in the United States and throughout the world.

National Association of Clean Water Agencies represents the interests of nearly 300 publicly owned wastewater treatment agencies nationwide, serving the majority of the sewered population in the U.S. NACWA's mission is to lead its member agencies in the development and implementation of scientifically based, technically sound, and cost-effective environmental programs for protecting public and ecosystem health.

National Association of Water Companies is the only national trade association exclusively representing all aspects of the private water service industry. The range of its members' business includes ownership of regulated drinking water and wastewater utilities, and the many forms of public/private partnerships and management contract arrangements. Every day nearly 73 million Americans — almost one in four — receive water service from a privately owned water utility or a municipal utility operating under a public-private partnership. NAWC members are regulated at the Federal level by EPA and at the State level by State health and environment agencies. State public utility commissions economically regulate these members.

National Environmental Training Center for Small Communities helps small communities with populations less than 10,000 by providing training, related information, and referral services in wastewater, drinking water, and solid waste.

The National Governors Association (NGA) is the collective voice of the Nation's governors; its members are the governors of the 50 States, three Territories and two Commonwealths. NGA provides governors and their senior staff members with services that range from representing States on key Federal issues to developing and implementing innovative solutions to public policy challenges through the NGA Center for Best Practices. NGA also provides management and technical assistance to both new and incumbent governors.

National League of Cities works in partnership with 49 State municipal leagues to represent more than 19,000 cities, villages, and towns. The mission of the National League of Cities is to strengthen and promote cities as centers of opportunity, leadership, and governance.

National Rural Water Association is the largest utility membership association in the country that represents almost 27,000 rural or small communities. Representing the best interests of the community's water and/or wastewater utilities is a core function of the Association. In addition every year over 50,000 individual field site investigations or technical assistance is provided personally to community's water or wastewater facilities. Combining these personal on-site visits with the over 30,000 attendees who participate in training classes conducted each year, the organization provides one of the primary means of communication to small and rural communities.

Rural Community Assistance Partnership assists water and wastewater utilities serving populations fewer than 10,000 people. Most activities are carried out in rural areas with populations fewer than 2,500 people, in minority communities, and in underserved rural areas with a high percentage of low-income individuals.

State Homeland Security Advisors form a network of contacts that the Governors of each State have appointed to coordinate homeland security activities.

U.S. Conference of Mayors is a nonpartisan organization of the mayors of 1,201 U.S. cities with populations greater than 30,000.

Water Environment Federation is composed of individual members and member associations representing engineers, public and private plant operators and managers, students, laboratory technicians, wastewater consultants, retired wastewater professionals, and public officials.

Water Environment Research Foundation is dedicated to advancing science and technology that addresses water quality. Subscribers include individuals and organizations from municipal agencies, academia, government laboratories, and industrial and consulting firms.

Water Research Foundation is a member-supported, international nonprofit organization that sponsors research to enable water utilities, public health agencies, and other professionals to provide affordable drinking water to consumers.

A3.3 Other Federal Departments and State Agencies

Federal Bureau of Investigation. EPA, DHS, and the WaterISAC work closely with the FBI to share intelligence and threat warnings related to physical and cyber attacks and to contamination incidents. The FBI and EPA prepare and update threat information related to drinking water and wastewater. Drinking water and wastewater utilities, as well as States, have been encouraged by EPA to coordinate security activities with local FBI offices nationwide. EPA has also developed tools and outreach documents to educate the law enforcement community about drinking water and wastewater utilities. It has offered Water Security Awareness training to the FBI's Joint Terrorism Task Force to provide an understanding of water systems, their vulnerabilities and current threats, and response measures.

U.S. Department of Defense (DoD). DoD's primary interaction with EPA is through USACE coordination; USACE is responsible for maintaining the Nation's commercial waterways and operates the dams and locks that facilitate commerce on inland waterways. A number of drinking water systems use dammed reservoirs as their primary water sources. Dam safety and protection is a critical issue for the Water Sector; some employees of the USACE Engineering Research and Development Center also sit on the EPA's NHSRC DSRC. Military facilities with their own drinking water and wastewater systems are regulated under the SDWA and CWA and, where applicable, must complete and submit vulnerability assessments to EPA.

U.S. Department of the Interior. EPA coordinates with DOI on dam security and water quality. Historically, EPA has worked with a number of Interior bureaus, including the National Park Service (NPS), U.S. Bureau of Reclamation, Bureau of Land Management (BLM), U.S. Fish and Wildlife Service, and USGS. USGS serves the Nation as a science agency that collects, monitors, analyzes, and provides scientific understanding of natural resources. In addition, USGS's National Water Quality Assessment program provides periodic assessments that include data for many potentially harmful drinking water contaminants. In part, USGS's monitoring and research programs support EPA's regulatory and research agenda.

Other DOI connections to the Water Sector are that NPS maintains drinking water and wastewater systems that are regulated by the SDWA and CWA. Also, BLM operates a number of TNCWSs (e.g., campgrounds), plays a large role in managing and protecting the western water supply, and some raw drinking water sources may reside on BLM-managed public lands.

U.S. Department of State. In its mission to create a more secure, democratic, and prosperous world, DOS collaborates with countries, government agencies, nongovernmental organizations, institutions of higher learning, and private sector partners.

It is critical for EPA to continue to communicate and coordinate with the State Department to ensure that water quality and quantity issues are fully understood.

Several major rivers used as sources of drinking water in the United States cross Canada and Mexico's borders and a number of Water Sector utilities in the Northwest obtain their treatment chemicals from Canada. It is important that the U.S. continue to work with our neighbors to the north and the south to protect Water Sector infrastructure and water sources from potential terrorist attacks.

U.S. Intelligence Community. The Director of National Intelligence coordinates the Nation's intelligence activities, and correlates, evaluates, and disseminates intelligence that affects national security. The U.S. Intelligence Community, including the FBI and the Central Intelligence Agency, engages in research, development, and deployment of technology for intelligence purposes, and provides an independent source of analysis on national and international concerns. EPA works directly with the U.S. Intelligence Community to ensure the flow of intelligence in support of homeland defense related to the Water Sector.

Appendix 4: Interdependencies/ Dependencies

Interdependencies between drinking water utilities and other critical infrastructure are shown in Table A4-1. The preliminary data gathered for this exhibit are not meant to illustrate an exhaustive list of interdependencies; rather, they capture many of the sector's broader interdependencies.

Table A4-1: Interdependencies Between Sectors and Drinking Water Supply

Sector	Sector Dependency on Drinking Water	Drinking Water Dependency on Sector
Agriculture	• Irrigation • Animal drinking • Facility cleaning	• Source water quality • Hydroelectric power
Food	• Food processing • Restaurant operation	
Healthcare and Public Health	• Hospital and clinic operations • Nursing home operations • Pharmaceutical, device, and supply manufacturing • Laboratory services • Sanitation services • Transportation of equipment and supplies	• Vaccination and inoculation • Information on treatment and response conditions for public notice
Emergency Services	• Firefighting and hazardous material spill and event responses • Emergency water supplies • Equipment maintenance	• Coordination with emergency responders
Government Facilities and Commercial Facilities	• Office operations • Equipment cooling	• Water rates and spending authority • Research
Defense Industrial Base	• Office operations • Equipment cooling	• Production of parts

Sector	Sector Dependency on Drinking Water	Drinking Water Dependency on Sector
Communications	• Equipment cooling • Common rights-of-way	• General operations • SCADA • Remote monitoring • Communication with the public • Communication with emergency responders • Common rights-of-way
Energy	• Steam generation • Mining operations • Ore processing • Refining • Pollution control • Raw material (e.g., hydrogen production) • Waste management • Common rights-of-way • Office operations	• Pumps, wells, and treatment; operations and repair • Office operations • Common rights-of-way • Repair and recovery operations • Delivery of components and materials • Back-up power requirements
Transportation Systems	• Office operations • Equipment maintenance • Common rights-of-way	• Delivery of treatment chemicals • Operations, maintenance, and repair • Delivery of components and materials • Company operations • Transport of emergency responders and equipment • Common rights-of-way
Banking and Finance	• Office operations • Equipment cooling	• Company operations
Chemical Industry and Hazardous Materials	• Manufacturing operations • Office operations	• Chlorine and other treatment chemicals
Postal and Shipping	• Office operations	• Company operations
National Monuments and Icons	• Office operations • Provision of public facilities	
Critical Manufacturing	• Water as a product constituent • Water for process support, such as cooling	• Critical manufactured utility components

Table A4-1 illustrates that most of the interdependencies other infrastructure have with drinking water assets are physical in nature; that is, these infrastructure require water to provide products or services. Geographic interdependencies seen between drinking water (and wastewater) infrastructure and other infrastructure are due to the practice of placing distribution systems (networks of piping), electricity lines, telecommunication lines, etc., in common corridors.

Table A4-2 demonstrates the interdependencies between wastewater infrastructure and other critical infrastructure. As is the case with drinking water interdependencies, most of the wastewater interdependencies are physical.

Table A4-2: Interdependencies Between Sectors and Wastewater Infrastructure

Sector	Sector Dependency on Wastewater	Wastewater Dependency on Sector
Agriculture	• Biosolids (soil amendment/fertilizer)	• Biosolids disposal
Food	• Restaurant operation • Processing plants	
Healthcare and Public Health	• Hospital and clinic operations • Nursing home operations • Pharmaceutical, device, and supply manufacturing • Laboratory services • Transportation of equipment and supplies	
Emergency Services	• Decontamination services	• Coordination with emergency responders
Government Facilities and Commercial Facilities	• Office operations	• Water rates and spending authority • Research
Defense Industrial Base	• Office operations	• Production of parts
Communications	• Common rights-of-way	• General operations • SCADA • Remote monitoring • Communication with the public • Communication with emergency responders • Common rights-of-way
Energy	• Waste management • Common rights-of-way • Methane generation • Cooling water	• Pumps and treatment; operations and repair • Office operations • Common rights-of-way • Repair and recovery operations • Delivery of components and materials • Back-up power requirements
Transportation Systems	• Office operations • Common rights-of-way	• Delivery of treatment chemicals • Operations, maintenance, and repair • Delivery of components and materials • Company operations • Transport of emergency responders and equipment • Common rights-of-way
Banking and Finance	• Office operations	• Company operations
Chemical Industry and Hazardous Materials	• Manufacturing operations • Office operations	• Disinfectants and other critical treatment chemicals

Sector	Sector Dependency on Wastewater	Wastewater Dependency on Sector
Postal and Shipping	· Office operations	· Company operations
National Monuments and Icons	· Office operations · Provision of public facilities	
Critical Manufacturing	· Manufacturing operations · Office operations	· Critical manufactured utility components

Appendix 5: CIKR Protection Initiatives and Resilience Strategies

Below is a detailed explanation of the CIKR protection initiatives (milestones) identified in Table 5-1. These initiatives are organized within the four sector goals which also correspond to the Risk Mitigation Activities described in the *Water Sector Annual Report*.

Goal 1: Sustain protection of public health and the environment:

1. Water Security Initiative. The overall goal of this initiative is to design and demonstrate an effective system for timely detection of and appropriate response to drinking water contamination threats and incidents that will have broad application to the Nation's drinking water utilities. The initiative is being implemented in three phases: (1) develop the conceptual design of a contamination warning system; (2) demonstrate, evaluate, and refine the contamination warning system design through full-scale pilot programs at drinking water utilities and municipalities; and (3) develop practical guidance and provide outreach and training to promote and support voluntary national adoption of a contamination warning system.

Currently, five Water Security Initiative pilots are in different stages of deployment in Cincinnati, San Francisco, New York City, Dallas, and Philadelphia. Using information gathered through deployment of the Cincinnati pilot, EPA has published three interim guidance documents on drinking water contamination warning systems. The documents advise utilities regarding the design, development, deployment, and use of monitoring and warning systems.

2. Water Laboratory Alliance. EPA is developing a laboratory network that is able to support the drinking water subsector by expanding its analytical capability and capacity to handle an influx of samples during an emergency incident. This nationwide network of Federal, State, local government, and commercial laboratories will analyze for standard chemical, biological, and radiological contaminants in drinking water resulting from all hazards.

3. Sector-Specific Metrics. The Water SCC and GCC convened a CIPAC Metrics Workgroup to develop a national performance measurement system for the Water Sector to assess Water Sector security and resilience. The Workgroup published its recommendations for voluntary measures for both utilities and "other actors" such as EPA, DHS, and States in June 2008. In fall 2008, the Water Sector collected and summarized utility and "other actor" responses to the first measures process. In fall 2009, the Water Sector initiated the second annual measures process to provide an updated baseline of information regarding vital preparedness metrics for all members of the Water Sector. The Water Sector is particularly interested in increasing the number of small and rural utilities participating in this year's effort. This information will be useful in comparing practices over time and between different size utilities, allowing utilities to assess their security status, gain valuable insight, and support the continued measurement process for the entire sector. Results of the 2009 metrics process were published in December 2009.

Goal 2: Recognize and reduce risks in the Water Sector:

4. Risk Assessment Methodologies. Drinking water and wastewater utilities are encouraged to conduct or update risk assessments as well as to prepare or revise ERPs on a regular basis. Three risk assessment tools are widely used across the Water Sector: RAM–W, SEMS emergency response checklist, and VSAT. EPA, DHS, and sector partners are working collaboratively to upgrade and revise existing assessment methodologies by using consistent vulnerability, consequence, and threat information within the RAMCAP™ framework, resulting in analysis and calculation of risk that is comparable within the sector. Revisions to the tools will also address the features and elements of risk assessments as identified in the NIPP.

5. WHEAT. EPA is developing a generalized (threat-neutral) consequence analysis tool, WHEAT, to assist in quantifying human health and economic consequences for a variety of asset-threat combinations that pose a risk for the Water Sector. The tool will analyze three different event scenarios—drinking water distribution system contamination, release of a hazardous gas, and loss of operating assets—and provide information that can be used by a utility when conducting a risk assessment. The tool will estimate the human health consequences (e.g., the number of expected mortalities and morbidities) for both the distribution system contamination and hazardous gas release scenarios. Economic consequences for the utility as well as the regional economy will be estimated for all three scenarios. A beta version of the tool including scenarios for release of a hazardous gas and loss of operating assets for drinking water utilities is available for pilot testing. Development of the contamination module and incorporation of data to support wastewater utilities is ongoing.

6. Cybersecurity Roadmap. The *Roadmap to Secure Control Systems in the Water Sector* (March 2008) was developed by the Cybersecurity Working Group of the Water SCC. It provides a ten-year, broad-based plan for improving security preparedness, resilience, and response and recovery of industrial control systems. The four main goals are to: (1) develop and deploy control system security programs; (2) assess risk; (3) develop and implement risk mitigation measures; and (4) improve partnership and outreach. Cybersecurity Roadmap milestones include isolating control systems from public switched networks and developing a cyber response protocol template; developing an operator control system security training program; integrating the Cybersecurity Roadmap with the Water SSP; and establishing a life-cycle investment and framework for cybersecurity. The Cybersecurity Roadmap is one facet of a broad set of Water Sector cybersecurity activities including control system security workshops for utility operators, a cybersecurity self-assessment tool, and information sharing about cyber threats by the WaterISAC.

7. Site Assistance, Buffer Zone Protection, ECIP Visits. DHS Protective Security Advisors (PSAs) conduct utility and buffer zone SAVs. DHS's BZPP is designed to help local law enforcement and CIKR owners and operators increase security in their "buffer zone," the area outside of a facility that can be used by an adversary to conduct surveillance or launch an attack against the facility. During SAVs, PSAs lend a hand in identifying utility vulnerabilities and security gaps and recommend potential protective measures. PSAs also conduct ECIP visits at high-consequence (Level 1 and 2) Water Sector utilities to assist in assessing risks, educating operators, and forging strong relationships in advance of events.

Goal 3: Maintain a resilient infrastructure:

8. Emergency Response/Mutual Aid and Assistance Networks. Water Sector partners are encouraging local utilities in every State to establish intrastate mutual aid and assistance agreements to enhance preparedness and improve incident response. The Water Sector has sponsored regional workshops and other outreach to provide information on how to develop a WARN program. The Water Sector is also pursuing mechanisms to share mutual aid and assistance across State lines if local and intrastate mutual aid and assistance resources are overwhelmed. Integration of WARNs with interstate mutual aid and assistance networks, such as EMAC, will be evaluated.

9. Training and Exercises. EPA, the States, and national Water Sector associations have developed tools and extensive training programs to help utilities enhance their emergency response preparedness and communicate with local first responders and public health providers during an incident response. EPA is providing training on the ICS and NIMS, which are national standards used by the Water Sector's first response partners. In addition to the ICS and NIMS training, EPA also has provided contamination emergency response training to the sector, most recently to wastewater treatment systems and their community partners. Sector partners sponsor tabletop exercises developed by EPA. The Agency also participates in national emergency response exercises and is designing an exercise specifically for the Water Sector that will test the ability of a major metropolitan area to respond to a major disaster impacting the Water Sector.

Sector associations also provide training and exercises to utilities and State agencies. The ASDWA hosted a workshop for State drinking water program staff responsible for water security initiatives. WEF, under a cooperative agreement with the Federal Emergency Management Agency, is providing a cross-sector interdependencies and emergency response training program to assist Water Sector utilities in building sustained, resilient local and regional partnerships across critical infrastructure sectors.

10. Business Continuity Planning. BCP is a risk management strategy that includes a variety of utility operation plans that collectively define how a utility will continue critical business functions during and after various incidents. BCPs provide the basis for the resilience of a utility's essential functions and critical resources, including key personnel and financial resources, as well as for the utility's flexibility to adapt human resources policies to meet the changing needs of employees. AWWA is providing updated guidance on the development of BCPs for the Water Sector and has sponsored several two-day seminars for utilities. AWWA is also drafting an Emergency Preparedness Standard for the Water Sector in the context of National Fire Protection Association (NFPA) 1600 (often referred to as the 2007 NFPA 1600 Standard on Disaster/Emergency Management and Business Continuity Programs) relative to the specific operational needs of the Water Sector.

11. Community Case Study Pilot Projects. EPA sponsored a pilot project in Seattle-King County, Washington to increase awareness of the benefits of implementing active and effective water preparedness programs. EPA and its planning partners documented active and effective security and emergency practices already underway in the community to protect its drinking water and wastewater utilities in order to share the practices with other communities. Expanding upon the Seattle-King County case study, EPA launched the "Chicagoland" Water and Wastewater Preparedness and Business Resilience pilot project, which focused on understanding the interdependencies of critical infrastructure and how an interruption in the Water Sector would impact business resilience and the economic viability of the broader community. The Chicagoland Pilot demonstrated how to integrate security concepts into daily operations in order to reduce risk and enhance business resilience during a water service disruption. The pilot projects promoted a better understanding of interdependencies between the Water Sector and other critical infrastructure, especially Critical Manufacturing and Healthcare and Public Health.

12. Community-Based Water Resilience Initiative. EPA is developing a community-based water resilience program to increase the overall preparedness of communities in the event of a water service interruption. The two primary goals of this program are to: (1) increase community preparedness through a better understanding of water interdependencies and a better integration of the Water Sector into community emergency preparedness and response efforts; and (2) increase preparedness and resilience of drinking water and wastewater utilities by developing and delivering tools and information that enable utilities to better incorporate security and climate-ready practices into their operations.

13. Decontamination Planning Strategies. The Water Sector has strategically developed mechanisms to guide future decontamination activities for the sector. The overarching strategy provides information, tools, and resources to enable the timely recovery and return to service of utility operations from all-hazards contamination incidents. It addresses a range of contamination scenarios related to the type of system (e.g., drinking water, wastewater), type of contaminant (e.g., chemical, biological, radiological), type of media (e.g., water infrastructure and equipment used to store and treat; distribution and collection systems; household plumbing; and environmental), type of incident (e.g., natural or manmade, accidental or intentional), and extent of contamination (e.g., concentrations, spatial and temporal variations). The strategy also helps to meet requirements for EPA under HSPD-10, which charges EPA with developing strategies, guidelines, and plans for decontamination.

14. Pandemic Planning. EPA supports DHS and HHS in preparing the Nation's drinking water and wastewater critical infrastructure for an avian or pandemic flu outbreak. EPA supports HHS by providing Water Sector input on pandemic and pre-pandemic vaccine and antiviral prioritization guidance. In addition, EPA developed a Pandemic Influenza fact sheet for the Water Sector. This fact sheet builds on existing language on www.flu.gov and other U.S. government materials and reports, and it provides links and other relevant information about pandemic flu to the Water Sector. EPA also developed a pandemic influenza scenario that will be included on the updated Emergency Response Tabletop Exercises for drinking water and wastewater systems. The scenario was tested in a pandemic planning exercise in EPA's Region 1 in September 2009. To support H1N1 planning efforts, EPA, in collaboration with DHS, conducted an H1N1 discussion forum with Water Sector partners in September 2009.

15. WCIT and NEMI-CBR. These two online tools were created to support the Water Sector in preparedness, detection, response, and remediation. WCIT is a comprehensive database of information for 97 chemical, biological and radiological contaminants of concern to the Water Sector. In 2010, EPA will add five more contaminants of concern to WCIT to address wastewater infrastructure concerns. NEMI-CBR is a database of analytical methods for chemical, biological, and radiological contaminants of concern to the Water Sector. EPA is updating links to methods and other information in both tools to reflect the most current data available to the Water Sector.

Goal 4: Increase communication, outreach, and public confidence:

16. WaterISAC (www.waterisac.org). This tool is a mechanism for all-hazards security information within the Water Sector. WaterISAC facilitates sharing of information about physical and cyber threats, vulnerabilities, incidents, potential protective measures, and effective security practices. WaterISAC is a secure, Internet-based, rapid notification system and information resource for gathering, evaluating, conveying, and sharing security-related information on drinking water and wastewater systems; communications are geared to utility executives, managers, operators, and security officers.